THE NOTES WILL CARRY ME HOME

Writings on Music
From Evansville and the Tri-State

Edited by Joshua Britton

The Notes Will Carry Me Home:
Writings on Music from Evansville and the Tri-State
Edited by Joshua Britton
© 2021
All rights reserved
ISBN 978-1-937668-05-1

Front Cover Art: "Philharmonic in the Amazon—It's a Jungle Out There!" Cedric Hustace © 2021.
Back Cover Art: "Philharmonic Sextet Recital" Cedric Hustace © 2021.
Cover Layout and Design: Whitney Arvin
Book Formatting Design: Paul Britton
Artwork by Cedric Eustice

Published by Bird Brain Publishing
Evansville, Indiana.

Bird Brain Publishing is an imprint of Bird Brain Productions
www.birdbrainpublishing.com

Summary: From the Evansville Tri-State, and for the benefit of the Evansville Philharmonic Orchestra, comes this anthology of writings on music from twenty-eight local authors. *The Notes Will Carry Me Home* is a love letter to Evansville and the arts.

ISBN: 978-1-937668-05-1

Printed in the United States of America

CONTENTS

Contents

FOREWORD

When the EPO hired Roger Kalia as its new music director, it also resolved to increase its presence in the Evansville community and to collaborate even more with other local arts organizations. The pandemic season of 2020-2021 made this difficult, but this initiative still got off to an excellent start, as you will read in Roger's piece in this volume.

I have served the Evansville Philharmonic Orchestra as a trombonist and as a staff member for nearly six years, but only recently did I become involved with the Midwest Writers Guild of Evansville. Bringing writers into the concert hall may not be as much of a no-brainer as having dancers accompanying music by Astor Piazzolla or showcasing artists during Modest Mussorgsky's biggest hit. But dissertations could be written on the many classical music compositions that are based on literary works. An entire orchestral season could be programmed using nothing but music inspired by Shakespeare. Many prominent musicians—one thinks of Leonard Bernstein, Aaron Copland, and Alfred Brendel—are also fine writers. It was with this history of literate musicians in mind that I conceived the idea of an anthology of music writings by musicians and authors with strong ties to Evansville and the tri-state.

By the time we hear the EPO's October 2021 concert, "Literature & Music," it will have been a little over a year since I mentioned the idea to John William McMullen at Bird Brain Publishing. John is not only a writer and a publisher, but also a music devotee among whose books are one on French composer Olivier Messiaen. A few weeks later, I worked up the courage to pitch the idea to Kimberly Bredemeier, executive director of the Evansville Philharmonic Orchestra, and to Maestro Kalia. To my great relief, all were enthusiastic about the project.

Perhaps an even bigger relief, however, was the outpouring of interest I received from writers. When I sought submissions of academic essays, personal essays, and poetry having to do with classical music, jazz, and the like, I was humbled to find how many were excited for the project, eager to submit their work, and supportive of the undertaking. As I was finalizing the roster of contributors, I kept thinking of others I could and perhaps should have asked. Among the writers—some I know very well, and some I haven't yet had the pleasure—are (unsurprisingly) a number of musicians, including members of the EPO; faculty members of both the University of Evansville and the University of Southern Indiana; previously published authors of fiction, non-fiction, and poetry; and four married couples.

The title, "The Notes Will Carry Me Home," comes from the last line of the final poem in this anthology. The line resonated with me because of the strong sense of community my wife Emily and I felt from almost the first moment after we moved to Evansville in August 2015. The rallying support I've felt behind this project, particularly from the writers, has only cemented my affection for the city. It has been a tremendous honor and privilege to serve as editor for this volume.

Joshua Britton, Editor

TWIRLING THROUGH TIME
WITH TCHAIKOVSKY

Mary Grace Bernardin McMullen

She remembered the dress
It had belonged to her mother
Muted blue silk
Covered in black lace
Out of fashion
So the mother
Gave it to her little girl
For dress up
For imagining
For childhood play
She put it on
And gave another old cast-off dress
To her friend

They danced together
In the darkened basement
Of her childhood home
To the strings of Tchaikovsky
On an old Victrola

So slow and lush
So melancholy and melodic

Twirling Through Time With Tchaikovsky

So bittersweet
So heartbreakingly beautiful
Emotional memories
Come rushing back
Serenade for Strings
String Quartet

And they danced
In their dress-up dresses
In the darkened basement
With just enough light
From a small rectangular
Ground level window
Casting just a few rays
Of waning sunlight
Onto a small patch of carpet
And they danced right through it
Ballerinas
And it was magical

BELOVED

Tony Brewer

*Beethoven used conversation books
to communicate with visitors, who would
write questions he then answered aloud.*

*I would rather write 10,000 notes
than a single letter of the alphabet.*

For the body is like Music:
life contingent on composition.
Your leveraged quill moves messages
from stimuli to awareness and back
in conversation notebooks I pass
to inquisitive visitors,
written questions addressed
at my most controllable volume.

And the body is like nothing.
Void absent the clarity of sensation.
Its windows closed and boarded up,
doors bolted barred and barricaded.

For I now sense a signifying tone
composed on the edge of madness.
Tiny and tinny and sounding
like a childhood tune lost
at the bottom of a deep dark well.

* * *

Art! Who comprehends her?
With whom can one consult concerning
this great goddess?

Who are you there, whispering out of range?
Hiding behind quivering fan
fluttering excited little puffs of wind
to cool reddened cheeks.
I see you and
I see only a long night's work
expanding imaginary spaces
unfurling before my mind's many eyes
like heavy foolscap inked and blotted.
Dozens of rushed fingerprints.
Yours I would have smeared there too,
unvoiced staffless notes interpreted
point by point countered leaving
behind effortless beauty where once
there were sleepless nights and longing
to extract and work out and refine.

Candles illuminating eyes unflinching,
unblinking ears that ache
to hear your dulcet tones, my dear.
My love in shadow a slow-closing iris.

* * *

To play without passion is inexcusable!

So we part.
Union of desire and devotion
ending in resolved, measured lines.
Not silence but rest
and the soft softer patter of applause
I must be turned to experience
pelting my skin like rain slipping
between cobblestones, lost.

O ocean of eternal abundance,
even your storms turn calm
concealing roiling schools and predators
beneath placid immoveable surface.
I return to my vessel,
my watertight mind,
solitary sailor in this raging tempest
of quietude
while you remain amid the breakers
of madness.

We share a rock that will not be moved.
The fisherman daunted by the rising tide
and you a myth.

* * *

True art is selfish and perverse — it will not submit to the mold of flattery.

And so Love is an art like Music.
Formal structure despite the seeming
mindless abandon of each note.
Each note building
the grand hall Music inhabits.
The hall a woman moved.
Her love a series of movements.

* * *

Ever Thine
Ever Mine
Ever Ours

You caught my eye, sly one.
But I cannot now lend an ear.
Not ever.
I have none to spare, not
even for Love, for Love
is a quiet thing unspoken

somehow present and diminished
aloud but held tight.

O tightly I hold tightly to myself!
what I allow myself to love.
The wind
Her skin
My music
slipping into great silence.

NOTES FROM A MUSICOLOGIST: A REFLECTIVE INTRODUCTION TO THE -OLOGY OF MUSIC

Christine Wisch

"Hi, Christine. It's a pleasure to meet you. What do you do?"

I generally do not think of myself as a shy or unsure person, but I am certainly someone who overthinks things, and being asked "what do you do" always sends me into a short spiral of questions, reflections, and analysis: Where am I? What is this person's familiarity with and understanding of music? With academia? Do they want a one-word answer? An explanation?

"I'm a musicologist. I'm finishing a Ph.D. in musicology."

There, I said it. My words are met with a blank stare and smile of politeness. Recognizing the uncomfortable silence and hoping to offer a conversational lifesaver, I follow up with some action verbs and attempt to answer more concretely the question of what I *do*.

"I study and teach music history. I also write program notes, and sometimes I do pre-concert lectures for classical music concerts."

You would think that after a decade of graduate studies in musicology and dozens, if not hundreds, of introductions, both within and outside university settings, I would have made peace with what should be such a simple introduction. But, as you likely have gathered from the existence of this essay, I have not. When I tell people that I was trained as a violinist, there's always a shared connection—almost immediately I begin to hear about instruments that my new acquaintance once played, or memories of favorite bands and performances. What does a violinist do? Well, a violinist plays the violin, obviously. But what does a musicologist do? How do they *do* musicology? What *is* this "ology" of music?

When I was approached about contributing to this collection, I was asked initially if I would like to submit an academic essay. Sure, I could do that, but I was struck by the premise of this collection: words and music as told by people connected to Evansville. I thought back on this past year and the many introductions I had made as I began to get to know the city as well as the many introductions still waiting to be made due to the pandemic. Thus, I took this as an opportunity to introduce not only myself but also the seemingly obscure field of musicology to a broad audience of music, art, and literature lovers. A short, anecdotal story about music and musicology with references to *Romeo and Juliet* seemed like a fitting—or perhaps poetic—topic for a book aimed at sharing connections between words and music.

Imagine walking through town and coming upon an antique bookstore. Intrigued by the window display, you pop in and take a look around. In the corner you spot a tattered box with an old, well-loved edition of Beethoven's piano sonatas lying on top. A music lover, you walk over and begin thumbing through the pile of various worn music books before coming upon a plastic sleeve containing yellowed pages of handwritten music labeled by the seller as music by Vincenzo Bellini (1801–1835). Intrigued, you take a closer look wanting to know more about the music you're holding and its past.

The above situation "virtually" happened to me. I was not in a bookstore, but rather, I was browsing through eBay looking for teaching materials, and I came across what was advertised as a Bellini manuscript. I studied the uploaded images carefully and quickly assessed the object for what it was: a handwritten copy of string parts for the overture to the Italian composer Vincenzo Bellini's opera *I Capuleti e i Montecchi,* a two-act musical setting of Shakespeare's beloved *Romeo and Juliet,* which had been adapted to a libretto by the renowned Italian poet Felice Romani (1788–1865).

Whose handwriting was on the page? I couldn't tell from the images provided, but I was 100% sure that it wasn't Bellini's handwriting and that the "Bellini" written on the first page of each part was simply a copyist attributing the music to the Neapolitan master, not Bellini's signature. Aside from the fact that such a likelihood would be incredibly rare, we can look to surviving manuscripts and letters from Bellini to compare handwriting. Such a comparison with Bellini's autograph manuscript (a work in the author's own hand) that is held in the Museo Belliniano in Catania, Italy rules out any uncertainty: the *I Capuleti e i Montecchi* overture was not a rare, one-of-a-kind autograph manuscript, but a copy made by someone else.

I reached out to the seller, explained who I was and outlined my observations. The price dropped, and I became the new owner of these parts. Sure, these pages are perhaps not as special or monetarily valuable as someone once thought they were, but we can still learn from them. I do not know where these parts came from—the seller had no information about their provenance and made no mention as to how they came into his collection—but I can make some educated guesses by putting the skills I've learned as a musicologist to use in what may be best described as musical detective work.

The thin, crumbling nature of the paper suggests that these are indeed very old pages. Gently holding them up to the light, I can find no watermarks to date the paper or begin tracing its origins. Sure, watermarks are far from being a foolproof method for dating a work or determining its authenticity, but they can sometimes be used as breadcrumbs in tracing an object's past. I know the piece must date from March 1830 or later, as that was when Bellini completed *I Capuleti e i Montecchi* and premiered it in Venice at the Teatro La Fenice. The parts I purchased came with an original, well-worn cover sheet written in a different hand and on a less porous paper, but there was no name. Fortunately, the inscription on this cover page offers a few more clues, as it reads: "Oevoertura k opeře Romeo a Julii as Beliniho." Some quick research helps narrow down the possible languages: the grapheme "ř" is unique to just a handful of languages, among them Czech, Upper Sorbian, and Kurdish. I follow my hunch and confirm that "opeře" is the Czech spelling for "opera." I keep going, word by word, checking that a translation from Czech makes sense. I confirm that "k" means "to" or "from" and that "od" means "by." Further research shows the "Beliniho" was an often-used adaptation of Bellini in Czech-speaking lands, while "Romeo a Julii" was a variation of the now-standardized Czech spelling, *Romeo a Julie,* of *Romeo and Juliet.* When I put all the pieces together, ultimately I have the title: "Overture to [the] opera Romeo and Juliet by Bellini." Closer inspection of the individual string parts reveals that the title is also written on these pages in Czech, but the music itself retains the original Italian directives and tempo markings, such as "Allegro" or "crescendo."

As a scholar who specializes in early- to-mid-nineteenth-century music, I find such details interesting, but not surprising. Italian tempo and dynamic markings were universally employed in music scores, but regional variations of titles and names are common. Italian operas—especially Italian bel canto works by composers such as Giacchino Rossini and Vincenzo Bellini—were all the rage across Europe during their time and in the decades that immediately followed. There is no reason this music would *not* be known and celebrated in Czech-speaking lands, especially during the mid-nineteenth century. What were these parts used for? The parts do not contain any performance information or dates, which is unfortunate, but again, not surprising. As researchers, we are thrilled when composers and copyists leave us nuggets of identifying information, but such details are often the exception rather than the rule.

Bellini's original overture was written for a full orchestra with wind, string, and percussion instruments. I can tell that the parts I received do not belong to this original version. A comparison of the parts I received with the original overture reveals a number of differences. For instance, the violins do not play in the very opening of the full orchestral version, and yet in my parts, all strings play from the very beginning. Why? In the full orchestral version, the wind instruments play an important role from the start of the overture, but this arrangement does not have winds. Rather, in this arrangement for string quartet, the strings must take on the roles of the "missing" instruments so that all melodies and harmonies are present.

The parts I received comprise a full string quartet—two violins, a viola, and a cello. This was a common instrumentation not only for newly composed pieces, but also for arrangements of popular works, especially operas. Prior to the advent of commercial recordings, individuals came to know music through publications and performing chamber music. Performance of chamber music in domestic settings such as private households and salons was common, if not the norm, for middle and upper classes throughout the nineteenth and into the early twentieth century. Additionally, it was not uncommon to hear chamber arrangements at public concerts—especially those hosted by music societies—when a full orchestra was not available.

How was this particular arrangement made? To be completely honest, I cannot tell for sure, but two possibilities seem likely: The first is that the parts I received were copied from an already extant arrangement of the work, one likely made by a publisher who recognized the large market for string quartet arrangements. The careful layout of the pages with even spacing suggests that this music was copied directly from a similar, if not identical source. Although publishing houses widely circulated works across Europe, it was not uncommon for individuals to make handwritten copies of exemplars they were unable to purchase for themselves due to scarcity. It is also possible that these parts were adapted from yet another arrangement, perhaps one for piano four hands. Piano arrangements of operas were also quite common, and it would not be difficult to parse out four individual parts from a piano score.

I cannot confirm the provenance of these pieces, but with the information I have gathered from the extant pages and my knowledge of nineteenth-century musical practices, I hypothesize that these pages came from a Czech-speaking area and were part of a personal music collection used for domestic chamber performances or perhaps belonged to a music society that lacked a full orchestra. With more time and access to international archives, I could perhaps look at contemporary catalog records, advertisements, or even diaries from Czech-speaking lands to learn more about how these parts were made and possibly determine ownership or specific performance circumstances. At the moment, however, these pages serve their purpose: they offer a tangible example of one way a musicologist can use her skills to gain meaning from musical evidence.

The skills and knowledge of a musicologist can vary widely depending upon both, education and research goals. My own interest in manuscript studies came from a month-long overseas course in Italy, where I worked with colleagues to help catalog hundreds of works that once belonged to a priest with an insatiable desire to collect music. The course served as an introduction to codicology (the study of manuscript books), preservation, handwriting analysis, and cataloguing practices. Such training has aided me in my own research in archives in Poland and Spain as I examine not only musical scores, but also handwritten letters and multimedia albums of poems, music, and art.

How did I come to travel the world in this manner and study musicology? My path in music began with the violin. A product of public schooling, I began playing violin in sixth grade and continued with it through high school, playing in not only school orchestra concerts and musicals, but also in a youth chamber orchestra and a variety of string quartet gigs. I went to college with the intention of continuing study of my instrument and earning a teaching license, but a broken finger from a freak accident just before the start of my freshman year slightly altered my path. I ultimately ended up pursuing two different degrees—a Bachelor of Arts in Spanish and a Bachelor of Music with an emphasis in education. I found that the music of Spain was woefully neglected in both of my degrees, and I wanted to learn more about it. I soon found myself preparing a lecture recital on the violin sonatas of Joaquín Turina (1882–1949). I read everything I could about him and the violin sonatas and realized I still had questions and wanted to learn more. Indeed, I had caught the musicology bug.

Countless individuals, societies, and schools have offered varying and changing definitions of musicology. At its simplest and broadest level, as the word implies, musicology is the study of music. Music, itself, is open to multiple definitions, and can be studied from a variety of lenses or angles, many of which borrow from other scholarly fields. Many of us identify as cultural historians who focus on music, looking at how and why music has changed over time. We may borrow anthropological and sociological lenses to understand music's relationship to groups of people, or we may be interested in understanding how music is or was perceived. We may study music as its own object, analyzing its construction, and we may ask what aesthetic values contributed both to its creation and its reception. We may look at instrument construction (organology) and try to ascertain the conditions under which a piece was performed. Above all, we ask questions and try to answer them using the skills and resources we have.

What can we do with the knowledge and skills we gain? Many of us write books and articles detailing the findings of our research, which takes many forms and covers an ever-increasing range of topics. Musicologists often specialize in areas defined by temporal and geographic boundaries (Music of the Italian Baroque, or Music during the Cold War), and within that field, they may be interested in certain institutions, theories, or processes such as choral societies, nationalism, or publishing. Although the field has traditionally focused on art music of Western cultures, musicologists find themselves working on ever-increasingly diverse topics, ranging from video game music (ludomusicology) to explorations of relationships between music and natural surroundings (ecomusicology). And yes, there are still musicologists who may specialize in well-trodden areas such as studies on Bach or Beethoven—although we may not find any new manuscripts or artifacts, we are constantly reexamining how history has been told (historiography) and looking through new lenses to enhance our understanding of music in its own time and in ours. Through publishing and presenting our research, many of us are advocates for particular composers, genres, or styles that have been overlooked or undervalued in scholarly literature, neglected by performers, and remain unfamiliar to audiences.

Similarly, we may prepare and publish modern or critical editions of musical works related to our research. Sometimes we discover works that exist only in manuscript form, or our research shows that a current performing edition needs updating. Often, critical editions contain not only information about the process of editing the music but also biographical and contextual information. In addition to looking at manuscripts and published editions of works, we may also look at treatises, letters, or manuals from the period to inform our editorial decisions. In preparing and publishing these types of works, we are advocates who champion these musical works and hope they will serve scholars, performers, and audiences.

Many musicologists work at universities, where they most frequently teach courses in music history and music appreciation. As instructors, we introduce not only composers, repertoire, performers, and instruments but also historical thought, practices, and aesthetics to our students. We teach students how music was composed, performed, received, taught, appreciated, and studied. We discuss tropes and conventions and learn to evaluate writings about music. Indeed, we want our students to come away with knowledge of the content we teach in our classes, but an increasing number of us focus on developing musical vocabulary and written, spoken, and presentational skills so they can express their ideas about music in effective ways, wherever their paths may lead.

Today, musicologists may also be found in a variety of positions and jobs outside of the university. Many work at libraries and archives, but they are also vital assets within performing arts organizations and cultural institutions, where they may wear many hats. Their knowledge of reception history or musical convention, for instance, might make them valuable members of marketing teams, where their attention to detail and strong writing skills are also used. Similarly, many work as editors or in publishing houses, while others work as translators, having developed linguistic skills through their coursework and research. We may work as radio program hosts for music shows, or in the concert hall, providing pre-concert lectures or even curating concerts and educating audiences. And, of course, we write program notes, too.

STAFF LINES

Jenny Kalahar

First movements are unrestrained, delicate,
a sweet, joyful bowing of a single violin,
its notes climbing to golden treetops,
tangling with breezes, then
gliding back toward our open stage.

A rosewood oboe curving into laughter,
rushing out to sea, then back in harmony,
is startled by love notes from a grand piano,
not too forceful, not too loud:
breathing calmly as a resonating melody repeats,
daring to kiss notation off a sheet.

A trio of flutes trills in,
lovely, glowing, overflowing,
matching note for note with grand friend piano,
retelling stories we all know,
not always in harmony,
yet twined, enmeshed, in the same key.

Staff Lines

Two brassy French horns, tendrillar and flared,
bend the tune into some strange waltz—
three-quarter time has never been this dark-hearted,
with swooping notes meant to interrupt.
We lose our beat, take time for breath,
and let these interlopers squawk.

Horns inevitably barge in.
Like city noise, they jar and jostle,
wanting more and more attention,
with overpowering, muscled hoots.
Those incongruent blasts and tuba blurts
shout and yell until it hurts!
How did this performance go so wrong?

The conductor waves the whole thing off.
He sternly points to us, his baton aloft,
and we straighten to begin again.
Our notes seem to write themselves on the wind,
black, inky birds quickly taking flight:
the tune a sob, an embrace, a stirring refrain,
then a trailing cadence, calming coda.

Standing to bow in electrified silence,
we leave this echoing stage together—
a scent of rosin in the air,
a trail of staff lines in our wake.

Musical Venues in Early Evansville

Kristen Strandberg and Melanie Baker

Evansville residents enjoyed an enormous amount of music around the time of the Civil War and into the twentieth century. Dozens of churches incorporated music into their worship, river boats brought shows to the downtown area, numerous bands and singing societies made up of local musicians performed at concerts and public events. Even traveling musicians—sometimes nationally or internationally renowned stars—performed at Evansville's many musical venues. This discussion will only scratch the surface of Evansville's rich musical history. We will focus on the venues and physical spaces in which music was made, along with further history of the Evansville Philharmonic and the Victory Theatre. Many of these buildings served as multi-purpose venues and sadly, many of them no longer stand. Yet their existence serves as a testament to a vibrant musical and artistic community in early Evansville.

Early Sacred Music in Evansville

The latter half of the nineteenth century saw an abundance of music in worship spaces. There were many churches of different religions and denominations that were established in Evansville at this time, including Baptist, Catholic, Methodist, Presbyterian, and Jewish places of worship. Music has long been essential to worship, and Evansville's churches actively engaged congregations through liturgical and sacred music (Elliot 27-29). Vocal and instrumental music were both considered necessary parts of divine worship, though much of the music was vocal (and sometimes choral) music, which had congregational responses and antiphons through popular psalms and hymn tunes (Butler 37-38, 141-145). After Evansville became a more developed and established city by the twentieth century, many new parishes (which still stand today) came about, along with new instruments, choir lofts and organs to aid in worship.

One of the many examples of sacred musical venues in early Evansville was First Presbyterian church, which was established in 1821 as the first religious community in the small pioneer town of Evansville. By 1874, the current building located on Second Street and Mulberry was built. The church currently houses a rare organ by the late nineteenth-century organ builder Edmund Giesecke, who lived and worked in Evansville, building dozens of organs during his career. Only five of Giesecke's organs have survived to this day. The Giesecke organ at First Presbyterian was originally constructed in 1897 for a small church in Wisconsin, but was sold to a family-run Lutheran church in Maumee, Ohio in 1962. The Evansville Chapter of the American Guild of Organists was offered the chance to purchase the instrument in 2016. The organ was purchased by First Presbyterian Church and restored with a new blower, newly resurfaced keys, freshly voiced pipes, and refinished chestnut ("Taylor & Boody Organbuilders"). The University of Evansville's former organ instructor Helen Reed was crucial in bringing the Giesecke organ back home to Evansville, where it was restored in her memory and is used by worship services today (Simmons).

Evansville's Early Musical Venues

The Apollo Theater, later known as Mozart Hall and the New Metropolitan, was among the earliest performance venues in Evansville. The theater stood at the west side of First Street between Sycamore and Vine from 1852 until it was destroyed by fire in 1883. The venue is not to be confused with another Apollo Theater in an alley on Third Street between Locust and Walnut—this Apollo was a saloon which occasionally hosted events such as laborers' union meetings and concerts. While the Apollo on First Street was not the most prominent musical venues in the Evansville's history, the theater was an active host to concerts and plays, as well as public lectures and meetings. The venue opened July 19, 1852, under the management of H.S. Stasser and by 1860 it was renamed Mozart Hall. The following year, the feud between the two Evans brothers marked an infamous chapter in the building's history. The brothers—the grandsons of General Robert Evans, after whom the city of Evansville is named—shot each other in a dispute at what was then Mozart Hall. Both brothers were killed, along with a bystander.

In 1865, the hall was remodeled under new management

to incorporate a larger stage and boxed seating; the updated venue was renamed the New Metropolitan. The building fell into disuse after the Evansville Opera House opened in 1868 and it was destroyed by fire in 1883.[1]

The Evansville Opera House quickly surpassed the New Metropolitan as one of the finest theaters in the region. Although the building at First and Locust was renamed three times and destroyed by fire twice, there was a prominent musical and theatrical venue in that location from 1868 until 1917 (*The Evansville Journal* July 15, 1921). The original Evansville Opera House boasted a large stage, orchestra pit for 25 musicians, gas lights designed specifically for the space, and seating for 1,000 patrons including a main floor, balcony, boxes, and a three-tiered gallery (Knecht 244).

The venue's early years saw many stage shows and musical events, but by 1875 the hall was already in need of repairs, with the *Evansville Daily Journal* going so far as to say that "the Evansville Opera House is a disgrace to the city" (February 23, 1875). Even with these problems, productions continued, showcasing everything from mesmerists to plays, lectures, and musical performances including operas, vocal soloists, and violinists. One performance in March 1878 indicates the variety present in many musical performances, as a Miss Babbitt performed operatic scenes and old English, Irish, and Scotch ballads (*The Journal* March 24, 1878). This mixing of high art such as opera with

---

[1] Special thanks to Tom Lonnberg and Terry Hughes for some of this information.

more popular musical forms was common throughout the nineteenth century.

After much discussion and several transactions, the venue was finally remodeled in 1890 and renamed the People's Theater. Prominent local musician and German immigrant Christian Mathias directed an opera to mark the venue's reopening (Elliott 205). Mathias had also directed an orchestra at the grand opening of the original Opera House in 1868 (Knecht 244). He was best known for directing several vocal groups, most notably the Liederkranz Society until 1883 and he was also the first organist to serve at the current location of Trinity Methodist Episcopal Church, now Trinity United Methodist (Elliott 202).

The original People's Theater was apparently a lavish venue; one newspaper article notes that the new drop curtain was a "work of art" (*Evansville Courier* July 30, 1890). The theater's grand opening took place in September 1890, with a performance by the Emma Juch Grand English Opera Company (*Evansville Journal* August 24, 1890). The theater, like many in Evansville, also hosted traveling minstrel shows in which white performers in blackface portrayed demeaning African American stereotypes. These practices were unfortunately common and persisted well into the twentieth century.

The People's Theater was short lived, as a fire demolished the building in 1891 less than a year after its opening, also destroying the *Evansville Journal* building next door (Knecht 245). Work immediately began to build the New People's Theater, which opened the following year. In the early twentieth century, the theater continued to host various types of shows, though it tended to support traveling burlesque shows while the upper-class productions instead went to The Grand—a newer venue. In 1908 the theater was renamed yet again as the Orpheum. The venue continued to host a variety of shows, including vaudeville acts—these popular variety shows included short skits, comedy acts, songs, acrobatics, and more. Image 1 from the *Evansville Courier* in 1908 comedically represents the allure of vaudeville and the way it showcased many types of performance. This particular show featured a virtuoso violinist, among other musical acts.

Image 1: A Vaudeville Show (*Evansville Courier* November 22, 1908)

Further, vaudeville acts often created partnerships with music publishers; performers would incorporate a new song into their show which would then be sold as sheet music as audiences left the venue. Interestingly enough, there were two music publishers in Evansville from the 1880s to the early 1900s: G.W. Warren & Co. and Charles Schmidt & Co. Both Warren and Schmidt were active area musicians and bandleaders. Image 2 shows a piece of sheet music published by Warren in 1875, written by Evansville composer Ferd Goslee, who composed music that was published and circulated across the United States.

Image 2: A Piece of Sheet Music Composed and Published in Evansville (Library of Congress)

The Orpheum hosted motion pictures and vaudeville acts until it was destroyed by fire in 1917. For nearly fifty years a theater had existed at First and Locust, but this time it was not rebuilt. In the meantime, two other major venues had already emerged as significant spaces for music and stage shows: Evans Hall and The Grand.

Evans Hall was commissioned in 1878 by Saleta S. Evans, whose sons had killed each other in the tragedy at Mozart Hall in 1861. Situated at the corner of 5th and Locust (now the site of the Children's Museum of Evansville) as the home of the Women's Christian Temperance Union, it held 800 seats and hosted a wide variety of events from internationally renowned musicians to politicians including Theodore Roosevelt (Knecht 246-7).

Image 3: Evans Hall (photo from historicevansville.com)

The year after the hall's opening, Italian soprano Carlotta Patti performed at Evans Hall, following much hype. Ms. Patti came from a famous family of musicians; both parents were singers, as was her younger sister Adelina, who is recognized as one of the great sopranos of the nineteenth century (Forbes). The excitement generated in Evansville newspapers preceding her visit demonstrates the degree to which everyday people during this period were engaged with opera and classical music. Most middle- and upper-class residents would have been familiar with the current operas and known the names of the era's major performers. The *Evansville Daily Courier* generated hype, making grandiose statements such as "[when it comes to] quality of voice, no one, living or dead, has ever approached her" (*Evansville Daily Courier* October 19, 1879). Following the November 10, 1879 performance, the *Evansville Daily Courier* reported an audience of over 2000 people, apparently "the largest audience ever assembled in Evansville;" since Evans Hall only had seating for 800, this could be an exaggeration or many patrons may have stood for the performance (*Evansville Daily Courier* November 11, 1879).

Like other venues in Evansville, Evans Hall continued to host a wide variety of events. In 1881, for example, a memorial service for President James Garfield took place there, featuring Warren's Crescent City Silver Band, among other local musicians. The hall was not used much after 1917 and was torn down in 1931.

The Grand was perhaps the most prestigious hall in nineteenth-century Evansville. Built in 1889 with 1,700 seats, including three tiers of boxes and two balconies, as well as a domed ceiling and huge chandelier, the impressive venue rivaled the opulent halls of much larger cities (Engler, *Historic Evansville*). The Grand's opening production was a performance by the Emma Abbott Opera company, who performed *Lucia, Bride of Lammermoor*—a popular Italian opera from earlier in the nineteenth century. In the evenings that followed they performed other shows including Verdi's *La Traviata*.

Image 4: The Grand, c. 1925 (historicevansville.com)

Numerous plays and operas came to The Grand. Not only did the venue host nationally and internationally known acts, but also local talent on occasion. Public events also took place at The Grand, for instance, the opening ceremony of a "German-American Day" in 1890, featuring several local musicians and singing societies (*Evansville Journal* September 13, 1890). Even an occasional concert of sacred music took place there (*Evansville Journal* April 24, 1892). By around 1910, the hall was mostly used for vaudeville shows and later, motion pictures. The venue was razed in 1962 (Engler, *Historic Evansville*).

In 1906, the Wells-Bijou theater was built on Third Street between Locust and Walnut at a cost of $60,000 (*Evansville Journal*, April 14, 1906). In September of that year, the *Evansville Journal* reported that John E. Mack, "well known musician and band master," would lead a seven-piece house orchestra for the new theater, known as the Wells Bijou orchestra (*Evansville Journal* September 26, 1906). The grand opening of the theater took place on October 15, 1906 with a performance of "The Ham Tree," a short-lived but popular work of musical theater which unfortunately included performers in blackface. Once tickets went on sale, the performance sold all 1,700 seats within just a few hours (*Evansville Journal* October 14, 1906).

The venue mainly produced plays, typically with live music. The *Evansville Journal* notes the performance of the opera *The Merry Widow*; this 1905 work by Léhar is more accurately an operetta, with spoken dialogue and songs (*Evansville Journal* November 13, 1909). Even plays falling outside the realm of musical theater would often make use of music for transitions between acts; clearly, the Wells-Bijou hosted a variety of musical and theatrical productions.

By the spring of 1916, the theater changed its name to the Strand, focusing on motion pictures. An announcement in the *Evansville Journal* boasts the acquisition of a $7,500 organ to accompany the films with live music—one of several common practices for incorporating music into film at that time (*Evansville Journal* May 17, 1916). The building was destroyed by a fire in 1926.

The Victory Theatre and the Making of the Evansville Philharmonic

The Victory Theatre hosts the Evansville Philharmonic Orchestra, Evansville's largest professional orchestra, which was founded in 1934. Originally opened in 1921, the Victory Theatre hosted comedy acts, organ performances, a ten-piece orchestra and movie screenings. After shutting down twice in the 1970s, the Victory Theatre underwent a nineteen-million dollar renovation in 1998 where it then hosted the Evansville Philharmonic Orchestra ("Our History").

One early roadblock in the development of an orchestra in Evansville was the ability of the community to provide training on all the instruments required to form an orchestra. The prevalence of marching bands indicates that there was instruction available for wind and percussion instruments and local pipe organists provided instruction on keyboard instruments. However, instruction for string instruments was a problem, since many string players are needed to form a symphonic orchestra, and the struggle to establish an orchestra in Evansville was hampered by the lack of string players.

Many of Evansville's residents had some musical training, thanks to Milton Z. Tinker, who served as the Director of Music Education for the Evansville public schools from 1868 to 1914. Tinker, a stern personality, insisted that grade school children be taught to read music notation and sing on key at the same time they were taught to read and write English (*Evansville Journal* May 3, 1914). Tinker himself helped try to form a symphonic orchestra in Evansville. These early attempts to form an orchestra were unsuccessful. Tinker's early instruction in the public schools taught choral music, and it wasn't until 1917 that instrumental instruction was added to the music program of the school system. In recognition of Tinker's accomplishments, the city dedicated the pipe organ at the Evansville Memorial Coliseum in his name. The Tinker Pipe Organ, in deteriorating condition, now awaits restoration at the Coliseum (*Evansville Journal* May 3, 1914).

Meanwhile, local organizations brought touring opera and symphonic groups to Evansville. By the 1870's Evansville possessed an Opera House, and the ever-popular marching bands could be enjoyed at Mesker Park or the Apollo Open Air Drinking Garden. In 1890, a group of Evansville Women established the Matinee Musicale, which utilized local musicians to provide programs of fine art music. The Musicale gave twelve performances each year and was modestly successful during its short life. In a few years, it too failed.

In 1923, Evansville again attempted to establish a symphony orchestra, called the Little Symphony Society. Johanna Hansi was one of the driving forces. The ensembled was conducted by James Gillette, the organist at one of the local churches, and musicians were drawn from the professionals of the theatre house bands and from the students of the Humphreys school. After two years of performances, this group also failed. The failure of the Little Symphony Society postponed, but did not stop, progress towards a full-fledged orchestra in Evansville. The ever-active Hansi developed the musical talent of the church into a performing group that was often referred to as the Trinity Church Symphony. After the death of Hansi in 1929, some musicians from the group decided to continue playing together informally. The stated goal of this group was to eventually form an Evansville Symphony Orchestra. The small group was to pursue this goal for nearly five years before achieving success (*Evansville Journal* September 24, 1936).

In November of 1933, the Evansville Philharmonic Society was founded as a non-profit organization. The Orchestra continued to expand by adding a pool of unemployed European refugees to its roster, and its performances were featured on national radio broadcasts (*Evansville Journal* March 24, 1935). However, by the 1940s, the Orchestra's roster had shrunk once again, due to the effects of WWII. Musicians who would have played in the orchestra during this generation were either involved in wartime production or had been drafted to serve in the US military. After the war ended, the Philharmonic concerts were held at the Memorial Coliseum; the orchestra previously had been performing at high school auditoriums and gymnasiums. Performing at the Coliseum allowed for a better acoustic space for the orchestra and for a larger audience of 3,000 people to be in attendance. In 1967, the Vanderburgh Auditorium (renamed The Centre, and later The Old National Events Plaza) became the Philharmonic's home, which was a much more modernized space for the orchestra to perform.

In 1998, the Philharmonic returned to the original space in which the Little Symphony Society had performed: the Victory Theatre. Newly restored at a cost of nineteen-million dollars, the Victory Theatre is the Philharmonic's home to this day. The restoration allowed acoustic refurbishment of the performing hall and a premium space to perform music in Evansville. Today, the Philharmonic consists of approximately sixty musicians, who perform a mixture of classical and pops concerts. There are two youth orchestras and outreach programs for elementary age students to experience the music of an orchestra. Today, Maestro Roger Kalia leads the Philharmonic in its 86th year of existence ("Our History").

Conclusions

Evansville's position as a prosperous river city spurred a great deal of economic development in its early years, creating the conditions for a vibrant musical scene. The venues and musical activities we've discussed are only the tip of the iceberg, providing a small window into the musical history of Evansville. We have, of course, brushed over many other musical spaces in this brief survey, including many prominent churches and other venues. The Coliseum, for example, played host to much more than the early concerts of the Evansville Philharmonic. Built in 1916, the Coliseum was a prominent venue for many decades; it is still standing on Court Street. In the early part of the twentieth century, it hosted a wide variety of musical and non-musical events, including Polish pianist Paderewski in 1924 and John Philip Sousa's marching band (Knecht, *Sunday Courier & Journal* March 20, 1927).

We can imagine Evansville's residents attending these performances, wearing their finest clothes to the opera, singing among friends at their churches, and performing locally-produced sheet music at the piano in their elegant homes along SE First Street. Middle- and lower-class residents also reaped the benefits of a musical community, hearing music during public events and parades, as well as the calliopes playing from riverboats. Further, many shows offered varied ticket prices and gramophones became affordable fixtures in many homes by the 1920s. Music was everywhere in early Evansville, setting the stage for many of the musical activities in the area today.

Works Cited:

Butler, Brian. *An Undergrowth of Folly: Public Order, Race Anxiety, and the 1903 Evansville, Indiana Riot*. New York, NY: Garland Pub, 2000.

Elliott, Joseph P. *A History of Evansville and Vanderburgh County, Indiana*. Evansville, IN: Keller Print., 1897.

Joe Engler, *Historic Evansville* site http://www.historicevansville.com/ Accessed 6/12/21.

Evansville Courier (also known as *Evansville Daily Courier*)

The Evansville Daily Journal (also known as *The Evansville Journal* or *The Journal*)

Forbes, Elizabeth "Patti Family." *Grove Music Online*. Accessed June 11, 2021.

Knecht, Karl. "Theaters and Entertainment." *The Evansville Story: A Cultural Interpretation*, edited by James E. Morlock, Evansville College, 1965, 241-50.

"Our History." *Evansville Philharmonic Orchestra*. Evansvillephilharmonic.org 06 Nov. 2020. Web. Accessed 10 June 2021.

Simmons, Denny. "121-year-old Organ Comes Home to Evansville." *Courier & Press* [Evansville] 2 Nov. 2018.

"Taylor & Boody Organbuilders (2018)." *Pipe Organ Database*. 11 Oct. 2019. Web. Accessed 08 June 2021.

Exactly Where I Need to Be: My Journey with the Evansville Philharmonic Orchestra

Roger Kalia

March 3, 2020. I received a phone call that would change everything. I still remember the excitement seeing the 812 area code on my iPhone. Three days earlier, I had conducted the Evansville Philharmonic Orchestra (EPO) at the Victory Theatre as part of their Music Director search in a memorable and thrilling concert of Mendelssohn, Kodály, and Rodrigo. I vividly recall the sense of camaraderie I experienced with the orchestra. I felt a natural connection and bond with the musicians, as if we had already been making music for years. The staff and board were personable yet ambitious, and the patrons and community were dedicated to the orchestra in a number of ways. I was the final candidate to conduct, and the silver lining to being last was the fact that I would not have to wait too long for the search committee to decide on who they had chosen as their next music director. Could they really have made a decision so quickly?

Prior to auditioning with the EPO, I had served in various staff conducting roles with different professional orchestras in North Carolina and California from 2013-2020 while also serving as the music director of a summer classical music festival in Lake George, NY. However, my dream had always been to be the music director of a professional orchestra like the EPO. During my student years at Indiana University, I had become familiar with the EPO and the city of Evansville. Many of my friends and colleagues at IU spoke highly of the EPO, but I never quite had the opportunity to make the drive down to Evansville and hear the orchestra myself. However, when I saw the posting of music director, I immediately jumped at the opportunity and applied. To be back in the Midwest and have the opportunity to work regularly with an orchestra of the caliber of the EPO was extremely appealing to me. I was also intrigued by the potential of exploring new programming with the orchestra and taking them to even greater artistic heights while creating a more direct connection with the community.

Over the years I had been a finalist in other music director searches, and it was my experience that one can never predict what will happen. As a conductor, you need to prohibit yourself from becoming too attached to the orchestra or too invested in the community during your audition week in case you are not chosen. I will be honest though; my heart was in it right from the start, and I kept thinking about my week in Evansville after the final concert. Perhaps it was due to the fact that I had spent four meaningful years in Indiana working on my Doctorate in Orchestral Conducting at Indiana University or perhaps it was the fact that my first job as music director was with the Columbus Symphony, a community orchestra in Columbus, IN. I arrived in Indiana in 2009 having quite a bit of experience as a conductor, but it was through the conducting program at Indiana University that I was truly able to polish my craft and gain substantial experience as a music director with the Columbus Symphony.

Three days after my audition concert with the EPO, I was preparing for a rehearsal of Dvořak's Eighth Symphony in New Hampshire, and I would be lying if I told you that the EPO wasn't on my mind. Fortunately, a few minutes before the rehearsal was set to begin, I received the phone call I had been hoping for. I picked up the phone and I was offered the job to be the sixth music director in the history of the EPO. Joy and raw emotion swept over me. I could not wait to begin this next chapter and had no idea how much the world—literally—would change in the week following this momentous phone call.

In hindsight, I am simultaneously amazed and unsurprised by the way in which the EPO navigated a year that no one could have ever predicted. I say amazed because of the tireless efforts and creativity of each member of the EPO organization—from its staff to its musicians, board, and guild. And yet, a year into this, I now know that such impressive efforts are nothing less common and reflect the ever-present support and strength of this organization. Still, this first year will forever be memorable, and its uniqueness merits reflection.

I would like to share with you what I took away from my first year as music director of the EPO, particularly the challenges that we faced during a worldwide pandemic and how we navigated through them.

The need to do things differently was evident from my first week on the job. The staff made it possible to live stream the announcement of my appointment as music director on both Facebook and Zoom. It is my understanding that the EPO is the first orchestra to ever host a virtual music director announcement. The fact that our staff was able to successfully make such an announcement possible during the height of the pandemic in a safe and creative way spoke volumes to me about their determination and resiliency. A mix of EPO musicians, staff, board, guild, volunteers, chorus members, and patrons from the community tuned in for the announcement. As I shared how excited and honored I was to be chosen as their next music director, I felt a sense of excitement and comfort. The support from these different facets of the organization was overwhelming in the best way possible. My wife, Christine, commemorated this meaningful occasion by gifting me a personalized mini-oak barrel for aging bourbon with an engraved heading that reads: "Maestro Distillery, Evansville, Indiana, Est. 2020."

Rather than having the EPO postpone or even cancel their season due to the pandemic, I saw the potential for connecting with our musicians using technology, particularly Zoom and Facebook Live. Often, as a conductor, there are few opportunities to converse much with your musicians as we are most often in rehearsals for hours and tend to retire to our homes immediately after, especially during the frequent late evening rehearsals. This first year, although we distanced physically, I made it a priority to host monthly virtual Zoom Town Halls with the musicians of the orchestra before the season began. We had about 50-60 musicians join us for each of these, and we were able to discuss a variety of topics such as the upcoming season and what we were looking forward to. We shared and traded ideas and I learned a great deal about the city of Evansville from these initial meetings. Perhaps most important was the bond that we began to create before the new season began.

My philosophy as a music director has always centered around orchestras being bridges to their communities, and now that I'm in Evansville, this idea is even more amplified and apparent to me. More than ever, our world needs orchestras that are active in the community and dedicated to enhancing the culture of a city through not only the highest quality performances, but also through education, outreach, and partnership. What makes Evansville special to me is its fiercely independent local culture, its beautiful downtown, its scenic parks and river, and an orchestra that has received both local and national recognition. I am fortunate that throughout the season we partnered with a variety of local organizations while also performing fresh and new works by living composers. One of my fondest memories of the past season was our opening Pops Concert at the Evansville Wartime Museum, which celebrated Evansville's contribution to the World War II effort and recognized our veterans. Another wonderful memory for me was having the orchestra perform at historic Bosse Field for the first time. Having the opportunity to conduct the EPO in the third oldest active baseball stadium in the country was quite meaningful, and the fact that we introduced our musicians to a new audience was even more so.

Collaboration is a guiding principle in pretty much everything that I do as a music director, and many of our concerts consisted of a pre-concert performance from different Evansville groups including the Evansville Horn Choir, tango dancers from the University of Evansville, and local Indian classical musicians, among others. The theme of "Connect and Celebrate" guided us every step of the way. To be able to dive into these initiatives during a worldwide pandemic is noteworthy, but to create momentum and enthusiasm around the community is simply wonderful.

To embrace your community, to listen to it, and then to make your decisions based on their voices is of the utmost importance. Success for me equals service to our community, and in the current political and cultural landscape in which we are living, it has always been a goal of mine to create dialogue and share the joy of classical music with as many people as possible from a variety of backgrounds. As part of the EPO's Diversity Series, our musicians were able to perform at the Tri-State Hindu Temple and perform works that blend the worlds of Hindustani classical music and western classical music. Just a few days later we performed a work by Indian-American composer Reena Esmail and presented a pre-concert performance of two Hindustani musicians from the community performing traditional Indian instruments. These diverse programs not only received an enthusiastic and positive response, but many patrons reached out to me about their desire to see and hear more performances like these.

As I reflect upon the past season, I am pleased to say that we were able to create something fresh and dynamic as an organization. More importantly, I strived to change the model and tweak a bit of the formatting to get a fresh perspective on what the EPO can accomplish. Every concert throughout the season featured at least one work by a living composer, as well as a variety of up-and coming guest artists. For example, the opening concert of our season featured a world premiere commissioned work titled *River City,* composed by Paul Dooley, which was a thrilling way to kick off our season in a work that celebrates Evansville and the musicians of the EPO. A silver lining of the pandemic was the opportunity to feature our musicians more prominently and perform smaller works that we normally would not perform during a typical season. I conducted our EPO Woodwind Quintet in a performance of Piazzolla's *Libertango* featuring tango dancers from the University of Evansville, and our very own Eykamp String Quartet was featured as soloists in Jessie Montgomery's *Banner.* Many of our concerts also highlighted members from our community who would join me in conversation on stage where we discussed their background and the impact that the EPO has had on their life.

The Evansville Philharmonic Chorus and their conductor Andrea Drury were also a delight to collaborate with. They rehearsed throughout the season, both virtually and in-person with strict distancing and masks on. Not only did we perform an extraordinary concert of Handel's *Messiah* (complete with face masks and distancing) at Trinity United Methodist Church for a live audience, but we performed a virtual Peppermint Pops concert in the Victory Theatre with the chorus situated in the audience and singing directly behind me. This concert was recorded and shared with Evansville hospitals, which brought holiday cheer and beautiful music to those watching.

Where does the EPO go from here? We overcame so many challenges this past year and I believe we became closer as an orchestra. As we look ahead to next season, I will take with me the various lessons that I learned during my first year as the music director. We could have simply called off the season as many orchestras around the country did, but that was never an option for us. For me, keeping the music alive in Evansville and healing people through our performances were at the core of everything that we did this past season. As an organization we took risks and tried new things, and yes, some things worked better than others. We received national recognition, but even more important than that was the fact that we remained locally relevant through it all. Moving forward, I truly believe that the sky is the limit for the EPO.

I've been asked countless times what my dream job is and where I want to be as a conductor in the next five to ten years. A typical answer is something along the lines of conducting the Berlin Philharmonic or New York Philharmonic and guest conducting the great orchestras. I still hold on to such dreams and future goals, but I recognize this incredible opportunity in front of me right now, which I would not trade for the world. I am focused on creating something truly special here in Evansville and building meaningful relationships in this beautiful city. I am of the mindset that everything happens for a reason, and I truly believe that *I am Exactly Where I Need to Be.*

in the quiet of the cave
in the silence of the world

Patsy Rahn

in the quiet of the cave
there are mutterings whispered
around the fire
the firelight flickers, shadow and light
chasing the sounds along the walls.

Outside in the silence of the world
rain falls, a veil of rhythm and
tiny staccato statements,
layered into melodies.

The wind, arising, lifts through the thickness
of the leaves, flinging and twirling,
rustling and rattling;
revealing the breathing
of the sky with its roaring.

in the quiet of the cave
in the silence of the world

In the cave,

hitting stone on stone, stick on stick,

clapping hand on hand, foot to earth,

the fire sparks and spits

the transformed wood sputters

and hisses—

bring in the flute of reed, of wood

divide the moment into

more moments,

a moving along in a flow of sound,

a flood of feeling, lifting an arm,

shaking a head, moving the mind

to imagine.

Listen and imagine what things there are –

    outside the cave,

    yet to be seen,

    yet to be felt,

    yet to be imagined.

Remember the cave drawings of bison, of horses,

running in herds their hooves shaking

the earth, a thunder of drumming

as the running flow of hot hides
snorting and blowing are captured
in a single elegant charcoal line
along the stone,
made alive by the flickering of the spitting fire.

Never tire of listening to the hum of the
stars, never forget to stand still
and feel the whirling of the universe,
then sincerely bend you ears
to the right, and to the left,
to above you and below you
and marvel at the march of ants
and the flights of flocks
and the rattle of clouds
scraping the clear blue sky.

What particle, what molecular structure,
what hormone and enzyme
do you hear when you lay in
the cave, the fire calmed down,
silenced to coals,
when the stars have quieted

in the quiet of the cave
in the silence of the world

and the roar of wind dissolved,
what pumping of blood
what beating of heart
what heart valve whistle
laces your closed eyelids
with dreams and imaginings
of things to come
that only you can hear.

A MATCH MADE IN HEAVEN

Fr. Jeremy King, OSB

Saint Meinrad Archabbey and Seminary was founded in 1854 by monks from the Abbey of Maria Einsiedeln in Switzerland. This mission of the foundation was to establish the monastic life in the United States and to serve the German Catholic immigrants in Southern Indiana. The early community immediately began the chanting of the official prayer of the Catholic Church. The chants were in Latin though some German hymns and texts were prayed during unofficial devotions.

A seminary school was soon opened and the formation of priests for the local area was prioritized. Teaching young men to chant the Liturgy of the Mass and other sacraments was part of the curriculum, and, in turn, these priests brought a basis of music to the parishes they served. We at Saint Meinrad continue to promote sung participation in the worship of the Church, not only in the United States but in other English-speaking countries as well.

In 1984 I received a message from our Fr. Columba Kelly, a former Choirmaster of the Abbey, inviting me to attend a luncheon meeting at our Guesthouse with Stewart Kershaw, the Director of the Evansville Philharmonic Orchestra. Maestro Kershaw wanted to invite musicians from the Saint Meinrad Archabbey, Seminary College and School of Theology to join the Evansville Philharmonic Chorus for a performance of

Ludwig van Beethoven's *Ninth Symphony*. He had heard of our musical tradition since arriving in Evansville, and he spoke highly of it. He wanted to tap into that tradition for the upcoming concert. After his words of praise, he admitted to another motive for asking us to join the Chorus. He said that he wanted to invite a large group of singers without adding any more women, since the Philharmonic Chorus women outnumbered the men almost two to one.

We were honored, and enthusiastically accepted. Thus were added twenty-five men—monks, faculty, and students— to the EPO Chorus. Dr. Robert McIver, a staff member at Kentucky Wesleyan University, served as Conductor of the Chorus from 1983 through the 1990-91 season, and it was under his direction that we began our adventure with the Evansville Philharmonic Orchestra and Chorus.

Our involvement lasted until 2004. For many of us, it was one of the most delightful and formational experiences we had ever had. Every Tuesday evening, carloads of us would make the one-hour trip each way for rehearsals. Dr. McIver also came to our campus to help catch us up since the rehearsals for the program had already begun. He was assisted by Mark Hatfield and later by Dr. Diane Earle. Dr. McIver was a very competent and patient director and always went out of his way to make us better chorus members. When we began rehearsing with the rest of the chorus, he made us feel welcomed and appreciated. Because of his graciousness, the members of the chorus adopted us as part of a "community" of singers.

The concert was a great success and we continued for almost two decades as part of the EPO family.

Maestro Alfred Savia became the Music Director of the Evansville Philharmonic in the 1989-90 season. It was during his time that we began performing in our Archabbey Church at Saint Meinrad in addition to Evansville.

The Chorus performed Mendelssohn's *Elijah* at the Abbey and then in 2004 Maestro Savia brought the chamber orchestra to Saint Meinrad for Handel's *Messiah*. Teresa Cheung joined the Evansville Philharmonic family as Assistant Conductor of the Orchestra and Chorus conductor in June 1999. She conducted the Chorus and a chamber orchestra for the Maurice Duruflé *Requiem* in our Church a few years later with the monks singing the thematic Latin chants. We performed the Duruflé both at Saint Benedict Cathedral and in our abbey church with Helen Skuggedal Reed as organist.

Joseph Eunkwan Choi became EPO Assistant Conductor and Philharmonic Chorus Conductor in August 2005. He brought the Evansville Philharmonic Youth Orchestra to Saint Meinrad and performed in our Saint Bede Theater.

The years that Saint Meinrad Archabbey and Seminary were associated with the EPO and Chorus were truly a blessing for us and we hope for the past and current members of this fine group of artists. The entire region of Southwest Indiana, and not only the city of Evansville, has benefited in countless ways from these fine musicians. As we say in the abbey: *Ad mutlos annos!*—Many years more!

Musical Roots

Alfred Savia

My wife, Kitty, often likes to play a game when we're with a group of people we're just getting to know. Being a musician (a violinist), she is curious about how others (usually in our gatherings, fellow musicians) not only got started in music but how they were first exposed to music. The question she poses is "What is your very first memory of LIVE music?" Unless they grew up in a house where live music was played by parents or siblings, often the response is "in church" or "when my parents brought me to a concert."

For me, it was not in church or at a formal event that I first heard live music, but in a home—though not our home. I grew up in a large extended Italian family on both my mother's and father's sides. While neither my father nor anyone in his family played a musical instrument, my mother's family were all musicians. In fact my maternal grandfather, Alfredo (after whom I was named and who died before I was born), was legendary as a virtuosic clarinetist. When he and his brothers— my great uncles, Pietro and Beppino—crossed the Atlantic to come to America they brought steamer trunks filled not only with clothes, but also with all their musical instruments. Whenever we visited my mother's Italian family in Irvington, New Jersey, there was always a veritable feast of pasta, meats, desserts, and, for the adults, plenty of vino. After the huge

Italian dinner, my great uncles would bring out their instruments—guitar, mandolin, trumpet, accordion and occasionally, the dreaded tuba—and play and sing—what else—Italian songs! Much later, as I began to study classical music and opera, I realized they were playing and singing not only the "popular" songs from their homeland, Neapolitan songs and such, but also popular opera arias of Verdi, Puccini and Rossini. What better way to accompany the sumptuous food and drink than a robust chorus of the Brindisi "Libiamo" from Verdi's *La Traviata*? What better way to say goodbye at the end of those evenings than with everyone singing "Buona Sera" from Rossini's *Barber of Seville*? This was in fact MY norm, the "live" music experience I had from before I was even old enough to remember.

When I was in fifth grade we had the chance to learn to play a musical instrument in school and got to choose which instrument to play. After thinking about all those choices, especially the shiny brass instruments, I decided on the clarinet. After all, I'd always heard about my grandfather Alfredo and what a wonderful clarinetist he was—we even had his clarinet in our house. I had no idea what a fateful event choosing to play the clarinet in my elementary school band program would be. It was the beginning of a career, a life in music, set in motion by learning to form an embouchure, learning fingerings, how to read music, and to count and play in rhythm. When I finally got invited to actually play in the school band, I was overwhelmed at the first rehearsal—how would I ever figure out how to play in synch with all those other players who had been doing this for some time. Little did I know that I would eventually be the guy up on that podium leading professional musicians through incredibly complicated scores in orchestral music that was far beyond my fifth-grade band soundscape!

My career as a young musician having begun, I put in many hard hours of practice, quickly securing my spot as Principal Clarinet in elementary school, then in junior high. While at Mt. Pleasant Jr. High in Livingston, I decided to audition for North Jersey Regional Jr. High Band but was warned that no one in Livingston had gotten into that prestigious ensemble in 10 years. Much to my surprise I made it in, and from the first rehearsal was enveloped in the sonority of an ensemble that truly played together, in tune and with a beautiful sound. I realized then and there what it was like to make music at a much higher level. New Jersey, being in the shadow of both New York City in the north and Philadelphia in the south, was a highly competitive hotspot for young musicians. This was also a crossing point in my life because being in North Jersey Regional Band meant I had to choose between being on the football team and being in Regional Band because of schedule conflicts. I chose music over sports based on the realization that I had climbed a mini Mt. Everest to get into that ensemble while I was one of many in my school to make the football team. And, while I continued to play sports—recreation league football and baseball through high school years and even varsity tennis—music kept pushing to the forefront as I continued to advance into the New Jersey All State High School Band and eventually All State Orchestra.

During my high school years I also got my first taste of conducting, having been selected as student director of my high school band. It was that initial exposure to leading and coordinating many lines of music, and multiple sections of musicians at one time, that led me to begin collecting scores and recordings. While still in high school I essentially started learning the basic orchestral repertoire. While sitting in the clarinet section of All State Orchestra, New Jersey Symphony Junior Orchestra, Livingston Symphony, or World Youth Orchestra at Interlochen, I always had next to my clarinet part, study scores, which I followed during long rests. I soaked up all this great musical literature with eagerness and passion. I'll never forget my first time hearing the Beethoven 9th Symphony, listening through headphones connected to the stereo system in our home—I was at the same time in awe of that monumental score and somewhat perplexed by it (partially because it was the enigmatic Furtwangler recording)—and I must admit I'm still both in awe and perplexed by the 9th. On hearing Stravinsky's *The Rite of Spring* for the first time, through the same headphones, I thought I was going to jump out of my skin!

When it was time to choose where I would go to college, I decided upon Butler University's Jordan College of Music. While I had been accepted to more prestigious music programs such as Eastman and Oberlin, I wanted to attend a school where I would be able to play regularly in Orchestra from the first day. I had visited the Butler campus in Indianapolis and was very impressed with the quality of the University Orchestra, having heard a ballet performance of a very difficult Janacek score.

When I auditioned there, I was awarded a full scholarship and was told that I would certainly be in Orchestra from the get go. I also observed that the conductor of the Orchestra, Jackson Wiley, was an extraordinary musician and inspiring conductor, one whom I knew I could learn a lot from. Little did I know how true that assessment would be, how much I would grow as an orchestral musician—AND how much Mr. Wiley would take me under his wing as a young conductor. He not only gave me conducting lessons but also gave me the opportunity to conduct the University Orchestra as well as the Indianapolis Youth Orchestra while he went into the hall to listen for balance. One cannot underestimate how critical this was in my development as a young conductor. Just as a violin student needs a violin to learn to play that instrument, a young conducting student needs to get his or her hands on an ensemble of live musicians to practice conducting. Not only did Mr. Wiley give me many such opportunities, I also formed a small chamber orchestra which played concerts on campus as well as in other venues, even touring a bit around the state. Eventually I became Mr. Wiley's Graduate Assistant in Orchestra and Ensembles while pursuing my Masters degree. During that graduate year, we produced a weeklong festival of music of Leonard Bernstein, and Mr. Wiley had me conduct Bernstein's *Facsimile* when we found out that Lenny would be in attendance. When it came time for me to audition for a very important summer conductor-training program run by the League of American Orchestras, Mr. Wiley made sure I was up to the task by having me run through the audition repertoire with a lab orchestra. I not only won a spot in that program in Orkney Springs, Virginia, but the audition also served as my audition to be Assistant Conductor of the Omaha Symphony under their Music Director, Thomas Briccetti. Thus in 1976, at the ripe age of 22 not only did I marry my college sweetheart (the aforementioned Kitty), but I also won my first professional conducting post.

While I did spend the summer prior to my year of graduate study in Italy, most notably in Milan learning opera scores under the coaching of Maestro Enrico Pessina (an assistant conductor at La Scala di Milano under Arturo Toscanini, Pietro Mascagni, AND.... Giacomo Puccini), my training was primarily in the symphonic realm. And with my appointment in Omaha, I was off to a very active career as an orchestral conductor for over four decades. From Omaha, I went to the Florida Symphony in Orlando as Associate Conductor and found myself suddenly conducting over 60 concerts per season for eight seasons (plus the expansion of our family by one daughter, Laura). After Orlando, I became Resident Conductor of the New Orleans Symphony under its Music Director, Maxim Shostakovich (son of the composer Dmitri), together with a final addition to our family, Juliana, who was born in New Orleans. From New Orleans, it was back to Florida, this time South Florida as Resident Conductor of the Florida Philharmonic for two seasons until (finally) I became Music Director and Conductor of the Evansville Philharmonic Orchestra starting with the 1989-90 season. During my 31-year tenure with the Evansville Philharmonic, I also served concurrently for six seasons as Associate Conductor of the Indianapolis Symphony Orchestra with Music Director Raymond Leppard.

My career as symphonic conductor also allowed me the privilege of traveling the world as I guest-conducted—in addition to many engagements in the United States—orchestras in Europe, Asia, and Central and South America (my five years of Spanish in school finally paid off since I could actually rehearse for my concerts there in their language). But while it was conducting orchestras and concerts that was the mainstay of my career, I kept being drawn to opera. I conducted a production of Donizetti's *Don Pasquale* during my early years in Orlando, and then served as Music Director of Orlando Opera for three years conducting Verdi (*La Traviata*), Puccini (*La Boheme*) as well as Gounod, J. Strauss, and Lehar, often with very big names in the opera world, including Diana Soviero and Roberta Peters. While I was far more experienced in orchestral repertoire, conducting opera—and the process of working with singers and stage directors—opened up a whole new world to me. The physical and musical challenges of conducting opera are, in many ways, more complex than conducting a purely orchestral rehearsal or concert. As Erich Leinsdorf wrote in his book *The Composer's Advocate* (for me the ultimate description of who the conductor is), any conductor with a modicum of training can stand in front of a major level orchestra and hold together a Brahms symphony. It may not be the most persuasive musical interpretation, but the orchestra is not going to fall apart! Put the same conductor in an opera pit, and the pitfalls will be evident from the first scene of the opera. An opera conductor must in essence be the glue between the pit (the orchestra) and the stage (singing actors in principal and chorus roles). The physical act of holding these forces, spread out over a large distance, must begin with a consummate knowledge of the opera score but continues with an unerring instinct for knowing how to lead all those forces in a unified musical expression—and keeping them from falling apart!

During my years as Music Director of the Evansville Philharmonic, one of my greatest pleasures was infusing opera into the lineup in many of the seasons I programmed there. It not only brought me back to what I had enjoyed so much during those seasons with Orlando Opera—the collaborative process of putting opera together with an artistic team of singers, stage director, stage manager, etc. It also introduced an entire audience in that community to an artform most of them had rarely—if ever—experienced. There was always a buzz during opera week, with patrons asking each other "Are you going to The Opera this weekend?" rather than "Are you going to the Philharmonic?" For me this was an evangelistic mission—one that I immersed myself in and was always rewarded by the successful productions and the audience's enthusiastic embrace of opera. For my final concert as the EPO's Music Director I chose not a big symphonic work, but a gala presentation of Puccini's last opera, *Turandot*. As I was winding down my tenure with the Evansville Philharmonic, I jumped at the opportunity to transition to a position created for me with the Indianapolis Opera (where I had guest conducted several productions already)—Artistic Advisor and Principal Guest Conductor. It was an ideal position for me as I would finally have the freedom and flexibility to immerse myself in a post where I get to work with a very talented group of Resident Artists each season. While my musical training has been as an instrumentalist, by this point in my career I'd worked with countless singers and stage directors, and am now able to help coach and guide these young singers as they step out of their respective music schools and embark on their own careers as professionals.

It has become apparent to me, as I am constantly re-energized working with singers and leading opera productions, that there is a reason for this passion. Hearing those snippets of opera arias and scenes from my youngest years, sung and played with fervent enthusiasm by my Italian great-uncles, is something that has stuck with me all these years. Whenever I conduct *La Traviata*, those carefree evenings of hearing that heartfelt "Libiamo" echo in my ears. And for me, those musical roots are ever-present and constantly inspiring the way I make music.

Syrah of Rhone and Cabernet

Nicolette Soulia

Syrah of Rhone and Cabernet
replaced my whiskey heart.
I once drowned sorrows within a shot,
but the glass became too tart.
Then I heard the sounds of jazz and clarinet
followed the tears of red,
along with violins, they say,
playing in your head.
I was told, "He's not a bad man,"
my Jack from Tennessee.
But Europe is a better place to live
and only slightly higher a fee.
So, jazz and cigarettes became my life
and maybe they all were right.
But Jackie's still standing in the corner,
just waiting to start a fight.

RHYTHM & SWEAT

Nicolette Soulia

Bass beat, pulse heat
Muscles contract
Release
Contract
Release
Contract
Re-
Repeat the cycle until you defeat
the pesky fat cells underneath
and maybe then he'll like me
and maybe then I'll like me
and maybe then I'll love me
enough to start to protect me
enough to save my heartbeats
for the one I can make the heart beat
faster.
I just want my heart to beat a little faster.
I want my heart to feel a little stronger
in the face of breaking again from another
one night stand lasting long enough for me to wonder

if it would ever heal me from the last lover.
Another cover
song sung in the wrong key
while I keep on searching for the melody
to match my off-key
harmony
to make me feel like a symphony
composed.
But I'm disposed
Decomposed
Ripped out of my chest and made to close
off my heartbeats from the recording studios
taping my voice with autotune and then…
packaged and sold for pennies on the net
to every little preteen
unseen
by mommy and daddy
filled with dreams
too saccharine
to hold dear.
Just another set of bass beats,
pulse heat
Muscles contracting then…
Release.

THE HEROIC SOUND OF THE HORN

Emily Britton

When I tell anyone in the general public that I play the French horn (you know, the one on Christmas cards, I clarify for them), I usually get one of two responses:

1) "Oh, that's like the hardest instrument, right?"

Absolutely, yes.

Or 2) "I love the sound of the horn! It's so beautiful."

It's always been interesting to me that the horn has developed this reputation of being so difficult; after all, pretty much all the woodwinds, the strings, and of course, the piano play way more notes than we do. Perhaps there have just been too many horn solos marred by what we in the business call "fracked notes." Although not a true onomatopoeia, you can probably guess what that means from the sound of the word. It is devilishly hard to avoid the fracks as a horn player. I think we get away with it (as much as we do) because of the glory that is our sound—that other memorable thing that people tend to bring up. I may be biased, but I think the sound of the horn is a very special thing: bright and brassy at one time, warm and mellow at another, and very often, to put it simply, EPIC.

If there is one word that has become ridiculously overused in our day and age, it is the word EPIC. Everything from a pizza to a hangover is labeled as epic, a far cry from the heroism and grandeur of Odysseus' voyage home from Troy, to give an example of a true epic. But the horn actually is epic, to the point that few heroic scenes in movie scores do not feature the horn. I would go so far as to say that film composers are the very best contemporary users of the horn. They get it.

Examples of masterful horn usage pepper the soundtracks to the *Star Wars* films (an actual epic), written by the one and only, multiple Oscar-winning John Williams. From the melancholy but hopeful ascending slurs of "Leia's Theme" to the heroic fanfare of the "Main Title," the horn plays an integral part in helping the audience know what's going on and who to root for when.

Horn players know they will get a workout when Williams is on the program. In their minds, they're not just playing the hero's themes.

They are the heroes.

It's pretty much common knowledge that Williams borrowed a lot of his orchestration technique from previous composers, mostly from the Romantic era, to great effect. One that immediately comes to mind is Richard Wagner. For many people, Wagner means winged helmets and oversized sopranos singing for five hours straight—yes, many of Wagner's operas are actually that long. Some of it is very complicated, dense material. But I have always heard that the best way to approach Wagner's music is through the orchestral portions of his music. Unlike many of his contemporaries, Wagner used the opera orchestra magnificently, tasking it with carrying much of the drama and emotional import of the opera's story. To do this, he assigned every little thing in the opera a motif, a small snippet of music that was heard whenever that thing or person came up. Williams and many other film composers snapped up this idea, which is why we hear "Leia's Theme" when Leia is on screen and the "Imperial March" when Darth Vader is nearby.

Wagner also loved the brass, expanding the number of the horns in the orchestra whenever possible and even inventing a cross between the tuba and the horn (the Wagner tuba) to fill in the gap between those two conical instruments. And true to form, in his operas, the horn gets to play the heroic motifs, from the Flying Dutchman's theme to Siegfried's mountaintop call. Of course, Wagner wasn't creating this association between the horn and heroism out of thin air: he was playing on tropes and associations that his audiences already had.

Wagner's native Germany was the cradle of the Romantic movement in music, and the composers of that era were often very adept at writing for the horn. They, too, called on its heroic powers, sometimes in the aggressive manner of Wagner but just as frequently as a softer echo of distant times or places. One of the common themes of the Romantic era was untamed and uncorrupted nature, and few instruments evoked this better than the horn. With its long history as a signaling instrument, heard echoing off hilltops and across valleys to communicate success in the hunt, safety after the storm, or the status of the battle, the horn was at home in the forest wilderness. A composer, then, could instantly evoke such scenery by including the horn, and nowhere is this more evident than in the last movement of Beethoven's *Pastoral Symphony* (no. 6). As the storm dies away and calm returns, the traditional "all clear" of the alphorn sounds. Though less heroic in nature than Wagner's horn calls, Beethoven's are nevertheless noble in character, and elsewhere in his symphonies, Beethoven does call upon the more heroic character of the horn, such as in the third and seventh symphonies. As he did with so many other instruments, Beethoven demanded more from the horn, musically and technically, than any composer before him and played a seminal role in developing the horn's heroic capacities. Once again, however, genius was drawing upon a previous usage and the audience's familiarity with a particular trope.

When Beethoven's predecessors were developing the symphony and giving the orchestra a life outside the opera house, the horn had already become a regular member of the ensemble. Most of Haydn and Mozart's symphonies use two horns, for the most part just adding another color to the winds. It must be remembered that the orchestra was still relatively small and the horn itself a shadow of its current self in terms of technical ability, but its sound still carried a particular significance to the audience.

When the horn was invited inside from the forests and glens of Europe, it was into the opera pit. As opera was developing and spreading across Europe from its origins in Italy in the seventeenth century, it naturally reflected the lives and interests of its patrons. At the time, hunting was all the rage with the European nobility, particularly in France, where various King Louises spent their leisure time riding after boar, deer, and other animals. Paris was surrounded by wilderness, as was Versailles, and by the end of the Middle Ages, hunting had transitioned from a necessity to a stylized, social diversion for the nobility. An integral part of this courtly (but still dangerous) activity was a complicated code of horn calls for various rituals and actions of the hunt.

An entire culture was built up around hunting to showcase the bravery of the hunter, and great prestige was conferred upon the best hunters. It was only natural for this favorite pastime to show up in the popular entertainment of the day: opera. A clever composer could evoke the hunt easily with the inclusion of a horn fanfare or two, and with that, the horn made its way inside and joined the orchestra.

In modern society, the vestiges of the hunt as a pastime for the rich and powerful remain in small amounts. Business moguls often make headlines when they book trips to Africa to hunt big game, but their sport is more often criticized than lauded. More frequently, hunting is a pursuit of the members of more rural communities. In either case, the pomp and ceremony, particularly the inclusion of the horn as signaling device, is far removed, but the primeval ideal of man versus nature remains, whether or not putting food on the table is the goal. The horn, then, has come inside permanently and transformed into an instrument vastly different from the one played on horseback long ago. The traces of its glorious and sometimes epic past, however, remain and inform the listener. Unfortunately, not all contemporary composers understand this: the worst offenders are those who simply see the horn as another pretty sound and try to make it do anything and everything any other instrument might do. The modern horn player can often reach that technical standard, but the most effective horn writing is that in which the listener can hear the distant echoes of the hunting horn and its heroic reverberations through the concert halls of history.

SINGING WITH THE SAINTS:
THE MUSIC OF ST. HILDEGARD OF BINGEN

Sr. Jeana Visel, OSB

When I entered Monastery Immaculate Conception in Ferdinand, Indiana, I had some awareness of St. Hildegard of Bingen as a spiritual writer; I had read her *Scivias* as part of a seminar on Christian classics. Once I entered the monastery, however, she was to become for me a mentor and model, as well as a source of songs that continue to connect us across the ages. A twelfth-century German abbess, prophet, visionary, writer, musician, artistic designer, healer, and advisor to leaders of Church and state, St. Hildegard was a Renaissance woman in the Middle Ages. Our Indiana monastery was founded in 1867 from German roots with our great-great-great-grandmother house being the Monastery of St. Walburg in Eichstätt. Thus it was not surprising to find images of St. Hildegard with her characteristic feather quill in our cloister hallway, in a church window, and elsewhere. As a strong, holy woman, St. Hildegard has been an inspiration for Benedictine nuns and sisters for generations.

Over time I have come to know St. Hildegard better, and I have grown in appreciation for both her solid theological underpinnings and the creativity of the way she expresses the Catholic Christian tradition. At the same time, as my understanding of monastic life has deepened, I also feel more protective of St. Hildegard. Because of her strength and varied gifts, different groups have sometimes appropriated her in order to promote their own ideologies. Particularly since the 1970s, second-wave feminists have taken St. Hildegard as a symbol of female power, and New Age thinkers attribute to her an almost pantheistic worldview that would validate their own. Hildegard sometimes is presented as if her visions came from some strange experience similar to being on psychedelic drugs. Her music has been recorded not only in Early Music settings that aim for historical accuracy, but also in a variety of instrumental and vocal arrangements, including setting her chant against atmospheric electronic music, or shifting it into rhythms set against techno beats. While St. Hildegard certainly was a strong woman, and advocated for a holistic approach to life, her writing and example are deeply rooted in the Catholic Christian tradition, and her music was largely created to serve the liturgy of a worshiping community. To lose sight of her context is to lose touch with the real beauty and power of her work. Conversely, to hold her circumstances in mind is to tap into wellsprings of deep spiritual richness while singing her songs.

Who Was Saint Hildegard?

St. Hildegard was born in 1098 in Bermersheim, the tenth child of the nobles Hiltebert and Mechthild von Bermersheim. This was a time of conflict and instability, a time of invasions and weather changes while nation-states were being born. Productivity was increasing, and cities were growing as places of urban learning. In the Church, corruption flourished, but also did various reform movements. It was a rich cultural moment.

From the time she was three years old, Hildegard experienced spiritual visions, but when she realized she was different, she concealed this until much later in her life. Some scholars have suggested that her visions bear a strong resemblance to some of the visual effects experienced by those with migraines. Eventually Hildegard would describe her visions as occurring not in ecstasy but with full possession of her faculties: "I do not hear them with my outward ears, nor do I perceive them by the thoughts of my own heart or by any combination of my five senses. I hear them in my soul alone while my outward eyes are open. I have thus never fallen prey to ecstasy in the visions, but see them wide awake, by day and at night. And I am constantly fettered by sickness, and often in the grip of pain so intense that it threatens to kill me" (DL 64-65, Craine, 36, Newman, 114). Whatever the cause of her visions, they came to be understood with coherent theological meaning.

At eight years old, as the tenth child, Hildegard was offered as a tithe to God, a pious custom among noble families. Rather than to offer her as a child oblate to an existing monastery of women, her parents made the radical choice to put her in the care of the anchoress Jutta von Sponheim. Jutta was of another noble family, a distant relative, and was herself only six years older than Hildegard. As a young teenager, Jutta became an anchoress attached to the reformed Benedictine monastery of monks at Disibodenberg. Others eventually joined Jutta and

Hildegard, and Jutta introduced the *Rule of St. Benedict* to guide their life together.

While Hildegard had no formal schooling, she was taught by the monk Volmar, who became her spiritual director, confessor, and later secretary, helper, and friend. In 1114, at age sixteen, Hildegard made monastic profession of vows. When Jutta died at the young age of 44 in 1146, Hildegard was elected abbess of the small community. Jutta had been a fierce ascetic, and it seems the two may not have seen quite eye to eye; as a leader in her own right, Hildegard emphasized moderation, and herself lived to be 81.

At 42, Hildegard experienced a "prophetic call" vision. While she had kept her visions secret from everyone except Jutta and Volmar, with this intense experience, she gained an affirmation of her identity and was told to speak and write. Hildegard felt called to be Wisdom's prophet in what she considered an "effeminate" and lukewarm age with poor spiritual leadership. She spoke out advocating spiritual goodness and truth in the midst of conflict between the empire and papacy, schism and civil war, simony, the Cathar heresy, the Second Crusade, monastic reform movements, the birth of mendicant movements, competition for endowments and relics, and struggles over the issue of clerical celibacy. Her first written work, *Scivias* ("Know the ways of God") took ten years to write. Writing not in German but in inexact Latin, she was assisted by the monk Volmar and a younger nun, Richardis von Stade. Ultimately her visions were affirmed by St. Bernard of Clairvaux and Pope Eugenius III.

With an influx of postulants and a need for more space, around 1150 Hildegard felt called to found a new monastery for her nuns on the mountain of Rupertsberg, near Bingen, about 19 miles from Disibodenberg. She met with difficulties from Abbot Kuno and the monks, and with grumbling from some sisters. Nevertheless, she managed, with financial support from the Marchioness Richardis von Stade, the mother of Sr. Richardis, and the Archbishop of Mainz. By the mid-1160's, her community had grown so much that she founded a daughter-house at Eibingen across the Rhine. Ultimately her original Rupertsberg monastery was destroyed by Swedes in 1632 during the Thirty Years' War; her Eibingen monastery was dissolved in 1814 during the secularization of the Napoleonic era. In 1907, however, nuns returned to Eibingen and refounded a monastery called the Abbey of St. Hildegard. Currently the community is home to approximately 50 nuns and is a great center of scholarly work.

As abbess, Hildegard wrote *Liber vitae meritorum* (The Book of Life's Merits, 1158-1163), a book on ethics about the opposing forces molding behavior. Her *De operatione Dei* (The Book of Divine Works, 1163-1174) is a cosmology of the relationship between humanity, creation, and God. It is believed that she supervised the illumination of the manuscripts describing her visions, and the images created are striking. Other works include *Physica* (a book of natural history), *Causae et curae* (a medical book), commentaries on the *Rule of St. Benedict* and the creed, and biographies of St. Disibod and St. Rupert. Hildegard kept wide correspondence with popes, queens, emperors, abbesses and abbots, nuns and monks, and laypeople, across various countries. Often she provided pastoral care to spiritual leaders, offering both support and confrontation by turn. She composed 73 liturgical hymns and sequences, which would have been sung during liturgies at her monasteries. These are collected in *Symphonia harmoniae caelestium revelationum* (Symphony of the Harmony of Celestial Revelations). She even created her own alphabet and "language," or at least a thousand nouns categorized into hierarchies of being.

In her sixties, Hildegard was ill for three years. Nevertheless, she was called to four preaching tours to call lax monasteries and clergy to conversion. She preached against the Cathars, who saw all physical matter, including the body, as being created by Satan. She also castigated the clergy, saying that their bad behavior was what had sown the seeds for such heresy in the first place.

Toward the end of her life, Hildegard's community became embroiled in a controversy with the Church. An excommunicated noble was buried in the monastery cemetery, and the Church authorities of Mainz wanted to disinter the body from what was considered sacred ground. The nuns, however, were convinced that the man had been reconciled with God before his death, and refused to allow it. The monastery was put under interdict for some time—they were not allowed the sacrament of Eucharist, nor were they allowed to sing their daily liturgical prayers. Hildegard protested vehemently to the pope and prelates, saying that by denying them music, they were taking away praise due to God. Eventually the interdict was removed.

Hildegard died Sept. 17, 1179 at age 81. Even before her death, people were gathering stories about her life in preparation to petition for her canonization. While she was considered a saint by continuous popular acclamation, her official process toward sainthood moved forward by fits and starts, and ultimately it was the longest canonization process in Catholic Church history. In 1979, on the 800th anniversary of her death, Joseph Ratzinger was among the bishops who petitioned for her to be considered a doctor of the Church, a special title for saints who have contributed particularly helpful teaching on Scripture and Tradition. In December 2010, the nuns of Eibingen wrote the same request to Ratzinger, now Pope Benedict XVI. Two meetings were held in 2011 to get documentation in order, and the process was finished in early 2012. In May of that year, Pope Benedict declared Hildegard a saint, and in October, she was declared a doctor of the Church, joining St. Catherine of Siena,

St. Teresa of Avila, and St. Therese of Lisieux as one of now four women among the thirty-six saints considered doctors (Ferzoco, 305-313).

St. Hildegard's Music and the Monastic Context

St. Hildegard was the first composer of her era known by name, and the first composer in Western Europe known to have supervised copying of her works. Her *Ordo virtutem* is the first known morality play. She believed music to be a form of prayer, connected with the celestial songs of angels, a space in which humanity could taste the joy of heaven (Kujawa-Holbrook, xli). She claimed that the words of many of her songs came from visions of heaven (*Scivias* 3.13), and her music was sung in her monastic community, and possibly elsewhere.

The style of Hildegard's music tends to be ornate, and sometimes long by current liturgical standards. Her work shows the influence of eleventh-century compositions, which tended to be more complex than Carolingian liturgical music. While she uses modality and some similar melodic phrases, each song has its own character (Fassler, 151). Hildegard's music often begins with a brief reference to the lower part of one's range, then leaps up to a higher range. As Margot Fassler describes it, "It is her love of this particular device of quickly changing register which gives her music its rhapsodic quality. The words receiving the leap are often key in the poetry" (Fassler, 164). Repetition is a key feature, as well as often using a main pitch around which the rest of the melody departs and returns (Fassler, 165).

The sheer range of many of her compositions is remarkable; songs span multiple octaves. St. Hildegard herself must have been a gifted singer to imagine such music.

Many of the poetic texts of Hildegard's songs, and a version of her drama, first appear in her *Scivias;* others later were collected into her *Symphonia armonie celestium revelationum.* While at least four twelfth- or early thirteenth-century versions of the *Symphonia* existed, only two survive: the *Riesenkodex,* which includes both *Symphonia* and the *Ordo virtutem,* and the fragmentary *Dendermonde* codex, which has 57 songs but no *Ordo* (Leigh-Choate, et al, 164). Most of these songs are addressed to God or particular saints. Imagery often draws on organic symbols such as blooming flowers, greening earth, precious gems, and birth; other imagery is Scriptural, with references to the story of Adam and Eve, the Lamb of God, and the virtues.

The majority of Hildegard's songs were written to serve the monastic liturgy, the round of set-time daily prayer known as the Divine Office, or the Liturgy of the Hours. Each of these periods of prayer typically includes a hymn, chanted psalms, sung antiphons before and after each psalm, a Scripture reading, a responsory, a litany or intercessions, and a concluding blessing. While today many religious communities pray just some of the periods of prayer together (such as Morning, Midday, and Evening Prayer), St. Hildegard's community prayed the full complement of the hours, including the night office, called Matins. Many of St. Hildegard's compositions were written to be sung as part of this nocturnal prayer. If her music seems mysterious and otherworldly when sung by day, imagine it being sung by night, when the rest of the world is asleep! One could envision the nuns cherishing this exquisite beauty as one of the secret joys of monastic life. On the other hand, the demanding nature of some of Hildegard's music might also have served as an aid in staying awake through these more challenging hours of prayer, especially on feast days, when the final responsory would be elaborate (Fassler, 175).

Other music was written for the mass, particularly sequences, which would be sung before or after the proclamation of the Gospel. While it is possible for today's Christians to understand the placement of this music in its liturgical context, some elements of Catholic liturgy have undergone simplifying shifts over time, and only rarely today might one hear a sequence sung at a mass. Moreover, before the reforms of the Second Vatican Council (1962-65), it was not uncommon for liturgical music to be drawn out and to continue in the background while the ritual action of the priest went on quietly at the same time. Since Vatican II, however, both priest and congregation are expected to be attentive participants in each sacramental moment, and music need only serve for as long as it takes to express each part of the mass; the next part of the ritual generally does not go on until such music is finished. Thus despite their original liturgical genre, many of St. Hildegard's beautiful songs do not lend themselves to a similar contemporary usage.

Reception of St. Hildegard's Music

In part because of today's difficulty with fitting her music into its most natural liturgical context, it is most common for Hildegard's music now to be experienced in other settings. It is performed in recitals and concerts, or recorded, often by and for those who may or may not have any actual spiritual affiliation with Catholic Christian spirituality, let alone monastic experience of prayer. By the 1970s, interest in in Hildegard rose as early music was becoming professional. The feminist movement also promoted her. As Jennifer Bain describes it, for feminists after the 1970s, Hildegard "represents a pinnacle of female power: she manifests a creative personality and a wide-ranging intellect, and wields considerable political influence. She seems so modern" (203). In 1982, Sequentia presented one of the first modern productions of Hildegard's *Ordo virtutem,* along with a recording. The same year, Christopher Page and Gothic Voices were successful with their recording *A Feather on the Breath of God.* By 1998, many recordings of Hildegard's music were available, with various interpretations and agendas (Meconi, 82; Bain, 68). While some of these efforts, like Göschl's 1989 recording of *O virga ac diadema,* aimed at the best possible historical authenticity, New Age presentations of Hildegard promoted by Matthew Fox and others often have expressed a goal of presenting her works removed of any historical or religious context. (Bain, 8, 28)

Without reference to the concrete act or spirit of worship, Hildegard's music can indeed sound ethereal and a bit strange.

Hence it becomes easier for those with little understanding to use Hildegard's music to promote ends quite different from her original purpose. I would suggest that whatever one's contemporary political or religious bent, it is important to know and respect Hildegard's context, and her intention for her music

> to bridge their earthly exile: to introduce a bit of heaven on earth, embody the praise of the angels, and place her reader-singers in the company of the celestial symphony. More than that, her songs encouraged greater faithfulness in cultivating celestial virtues and renouncing the devil.... To sing the liturgy... was to unite soul and body in emulation and adoration of Christ. It was to join in the supernal 'song of rejoicing, sung in consonance and in concord, [which] tells of the glory and honor of the citizens of Heaven, and lifts on high what the Word has shown (Leigh-Choate, et al, 192; cf. *Scivias* 3.13.11).

Beauty can lead people to reflect on truth and goodness. For Saint Hildegard, the beauty of her music was meant to promote the love of God and growth in Christian virtue. Indeed, virtues are a major theme across her various works. Hildegard was a woman of her place and time, and while her music does have timeless power, it was written with an expressly Christian purpose. To use it carelessly for other ends is to risk distorting the truth of who she was and what she stood for.

Works Cited:

Bain, Jennifer. *Hildegard of Bingen and Musical Reception: The Modern Revival of a Medieval Composer*. Cambridge: Cambridge University Press, 2015.

Craine, Renate. *Hildegard: Prophet of the Cosmic Christ*. New York: Crossroad, 1997.

Fassler, Margot. "Composer and Dramatist: 'Melodious Singing and the Freshness of Remorse'," in Barbara Newman, ed., *Voice of the Living Light: Hildegard of Bingen and her World*, 149-175. Berkeley and LA: University of California Press, 1998.

Ferzoco, George. "The Canonization and Doctorization of Hildegard of Bingen," in Beverly Mayne Kienzle, Debra Stoudt, and George Ferzoco, eds. *A Companion to Hildegard of Bingen*, 305-316. Boston: Brill, 2014.

Kujawa-Holbrook, Sheryl. *Hildegard of Bingen: Essential Writings and Chants of a Christian Mystic- Annotated and Explained*. Woodstock, VT: SkyLight Paths Publishing, 2016.

Leigh-Choate, Tova, William T. Flynn, and Margot Fassler. "Hearing the Heavenly Symphony: An Overview of Hildegard's Musical Oeuvre with Case Studies," in Beverly Mayne Kienzle, Debra Stoudt, and George Ferzoco, eds. *A Companion to Hildegard of Bingen*, 163-192. Boston: Brill, 2014.

Meconi, Honey. *Hildegard of Bingen*. Urbana, Springfield, and Chicago: University of Illinois Press, 2018.

Other Sources:

Bowie, Fiona and Oliver Davies, eds. *Hildegard of Bingen: Mystical Writings*. Trans. Robert Carver. New York: Crossroad, 1990.

Gottfried of Disibodenberg and Theodoric of Echternach. *The Life of Saintly Hildegard*. Trans. Hugh Feiss. Toronto: Peregrina Publishing, 1996.

St. Hildegard of Bingen. *Scivias*. Trans. Mother Columba Hart and Jane Bishop. Mahwah, NJ: Paulist, 1990.

_____. *Symphonia: A Critical Edition of the Symphonia armonie celestium revelationum* [Symphony of the Harmony of Celestial Revelations]. Trans. Barbara Newman. Ithaca, NY: Cornell University Press, 1988.

_____. *The Book of Divine Works*. Trans. Nathaniel Campbell. Washington, DC: Catholic University of America Press, 2018.

_____. *The Book of the Rewards of Life (Liber Vitae Meritorum)*. Trans. Bruce Hozeski. New York and London: Garland, 1994.

_____. *The Letters of Hildegard of Bingen, Volume 2*. Trans. Joseph Baird and Radd Ehrman. New York and Oxford: Oxford University Press, 1998.

CHANTS OF ETERNITY

Patrick Kalahar

I was a pilgrim,
a pilgrim with a destination
but without a purpose.
Scaling a narrow outcrop
of the Bavarian Alps alone
in the early spring,
I climbed toward the light—
bright and burning,
winter pallor seared from flesh
in the thin mountain air.

The rising walls of jagged stone
were hot and dry, but the
rifts and ravines were
filled with snow a meter deep.
Foolishly, I followed none
of the many trails, and often
my way was barred by
newborn streams of melted snow,

forcing me to find another direction.
I was lost with no way back.

I had to go on. The icy waters
sometimes bubbling and churning
in rising and diminishing waves of sound
like the voices of a multitude, sometimes
thundering defiance like demons,
alternately spoke of beauty and then despair.
Death seemed a real possibility.
Suddenly, I reached the peak
and looked down onto the plain,
bright and radiant with magical light,

The goal I thought I would never see—
Kloster Ettal, the Baroque monastery.
Black domed, blinding white and
every detail gilded, set in a sea
of grass impossibly green.
I climbed down an easy and well-worn path
and entered the monastery.
Total darkness, and singing that I felt
in my bones and in the tingling of my nerves,
and tears of profound joy.

Deliverance from struggle and terror
to ecstasy and a vision of possibility.
The monks were chanting the liturgy
and the Veneration of the Saints.
The sounds rolled and echoed off the walls
in rising and diminishing waves of sound.
The voices of a multitude, call and response,
beauty and the end of despair.
My eyes adjusted.

At last I could see the light.

.

WITHHOLDING SAX

Tony Brewer

You do not get to have jazz in the woods
which is not to say the instruments cease to exist
or the concept migrates to "home" like dark birds of prey
to ledges of concrete edifices & the squeal of innocent subways
as if a music come up in fields
now refined only sits up straight at table
orders its own damn scotch and soda
applauding a heretofore unknowable unknown
sits cool in a suit straightening its tie
brushing cigarette ash off its lapel
feeling the heat and the press
of a gyrating if only in their minds crowd
moments before/after taking a late night stage
club owner short changes even stiffs
but out there man out there on the edge of a blade
cutting the air in so many savage sensual ways
I'm just saying you might not appreciate it so much in the woods
might be better off listening to something else

CLASSICAL MUSIC IN THE FILMS OF STANLEY KUBRICK

Joshua Britton

The main musical theme to *2001: A Space Odyssey* is often programmed on science-fiction-themed orchestral concerts like the Evansville Philharmonic Orchestra's 2019 Young People's Concerts, which also included Holst's *The Planets* and *Star Wars*. Because of John Williams's success with *Star Wars*, *E.T.*, and *Close Encounters of the Third Kind*, among other films whose themes are often included on similar concerts, listeners often incorrectly attribute the music in *2001* to him. But John Williams was primarily a television composer throughout the sixties and had no involvement with Stanley Kubrick's film, which was released in 1968.

Instead, Kubrick had turned to Alex North, with whom he had collaborated on *Spartacus* several years earlier, to write the music for his new film. But when North attended the premiere of *2001*, he was devastated to find that his entire score had been cut from the film. In its place was previously composed concert hall music by Richard Strauss, Johann Strauss Jr., and György Ligeti. Thus began Kubrick's practice of primarily using previously composed music for his films.

Kubrick was a notorious control freak, even more so as his reputation and eccentricities grew. Yet he preferred to work with pre-existing material as a jumping off point. Almost all of his movies—*Lolita, Barry Lyndon, A Clockwork Orange*—were based on a book or short story. Even with *2001*, Kubrick reached out to science-fiction writer Arthur C. Clarke, singled out several of Clarke's stories, and told him that he wanted to make a film like them. Kubrick did the same with sets; rather than leave the building of the interior of the Overlook Hotel in *The Shining* to the imagination of a production designer, Kubrick borrowed ideas from photographs of pre-existing hotels, saying he wanted the carpet to be like this one, the walls to be like that one, and the ballroom to look like another. Nor was Kubrick shy about taking control of the cinematography, either, as evidenced by the famous clip from the making of *The Shining* that shows him lying on the ground underneath his lead actor, camera in hand, directing him while shooting at an upward angle.

But unlike film directors John Carpenter (*Halloween, Escape From New York*) and Robert Rodriguez (*Sin City, Once Upon a Time in Mexico*), who moonlight as musicians and write music for their own films, Kubrick's talents did not extend to musical composition. He knew that he would have to rely on somebody else to write the music. Or did he?

2001 followed *Dr. Strangelove* in the filmmaker's filmography. Audiences immediately noticed a stark visual contrast—black and white versus color—and in subject matter—cold war versus outer space. Perhaps the biggest difference, though, was in the way *2001* sounded—far less dialogue, much more music:

in *Dr. Strangelove*, except for the beginning and end credits, there is little music other than a sparsely orchestrated version of "When Johnny Comes Marching Home," heard during the bomb run sequences.

It's not uncommon for film scripts to specify music that should be playing during particular scenes and over specific dialogue. Original film scores are generally not completed until post-production. But if a director uses previously written and recorded music, he necessarily makes that decision ahead of time and knows what music will be heard during any given scene while it is being filmed. It is surprising, therefore, that somebody as meticulous as Kubrick could have been so indecisive about the music for *2001*, a film many people would later consider his masterpiece, that he would dramatically change course so late in the production process.

Perhaps Kubrick, in his dissatisfaction with North's score, had an epiphany: that the floating translucent fetus in the final images of the film represented the birth of a sort of superman (not the comic book hero). And perhaps somebody mentioned to him the philosophical work by Friedrich Nietzsche, *Also Sprach Zarathustra* (*Thus Spake Zarathustra*), published in installments from 1883-1885, and its discussion of the *Übermensch*, or *superman*. And perhaps someone else mentioned Richard Strauss's 1896 tone poem based on the Nietzsche work.

Regardless, *Also Sprach Zarathustra* is the piece of music most associated with *2001: A Space Odyssey*. A short excerpt from the tone poem is used three times in the film: for the opening credits, a sunrise; at the end of the *Dawn of Man* sequence when Moonwatcher, the main ape, realizes he can use a bone as a weapon; and at the end, just before the end credits, with the appearance of the fetus.

Concertgoers aware of this excerpt's use in Kubrick's film are sometimes surprised to learn that Strauss's composition is actually thirty-five minutes long and includes much more than the minute and forty-five seconds of music heard in the movie. There are multiple recurring themes throughout the piece, including the first three-note theme (*do, sol,* and *do* up an octave), though this theme (representing the sun, earth, and moon) recurs much more subtly than the beginning, with one blatant exception (approximately eight minutes in).

The actual beginning of the film, however, which is omitted from some home video versions, consists of several minutes of a completely blank screen while György Ligeti's micropolyphonic work, *Atmospheres,* is heard. This happens again during the "built-in" intermission of the film: blank screen, same piece. Unlike Steven Spielberg with John Williams, Sergio Leone with Ennio Morricone, and Alfred Hitchcock with Bernard Hermann, Kubrick did not have a long-time collaboration with a film composer. But while Ligeti did not compose music specifically for film, one could argue that Ligeti was Kubrick's composer of choice. Not only was *Atmospheres* prominently featured multiple times throughout *2001*, but so was what is perhaps Ligeti's most famous work, *Lux Aeterna,* as well as *Aventures,* and the "Kyrie" from his *Requiem.* Kubrick also used Ligeti's music later in *The Shining* and *Eyes Wide Shut.*

In Kubrick's films, beginning with *2001,* the music is consistently in the forefront and is as important, if not more so, as the camera angles, the dialogue, and the expressions on the actors' faces. Some of Kubrick's contemporaries have gone to the opposite extreme. Sydney Lumet, for instance, fought to use as little music as possible in *Serpico*, and in his follow-up, *Dog Day Afternoon*, music is played only during the first few introductory minutes, and not again for the rest of the movie, not even during the closing credits.

Christopher Nolan's films too lack melodic content. While there's a lot of music in his third film, *Insomnia*, it seems to consist almost entirely of one sustained chord after another. Even the scores for his later larger-scale films, which were composed by Hans Zimmer, still consist largely of mood music and minimalistic *Jaws*-like ostinatos, such as the recognizable *Batman Begins* theme, with little resembling a hummable melody.

2001, on the other hand, was referred to as "an opera" by Kubrick's biographer, John Baxter, while *Star Wars* director George Lucas described the cinematography of *2001* by saying "all of the shots are very long and very slow and very musical." There is virtually no dialogue or any other sound while music is heard.

One might describe the music in *The Shining* as "mood" music. For *The Shining*, Kubrick borrowed from Krzystzof Penderecki and Bela Bartok as well as from Ligeti. Except for Wendy Carlos's electronic arrangement of the *Dies Irae*, *The Shining* does not feature the kind of music that will get stuck in your head.

But where the music in *Insomnia* may go largely unnoticed, Ligeti's unhummable music in *2001* is more than just an effect. For instance, when the scientists finally land on the moon to observe the monolith, Ligeti's *Lux Aeterna* merges with the "Kyrie" as the scientists gather to have their picture taken in front of it, upon which they are interrupted by a high-pitched feedback-like shriek. While viewers may not remember this as "actual music," they will surely remember what the moment felt and sounded like.

And Ligeti's music shines even more prominently during the third and final act of the movie. "Jupiter and Beyond the Total Infinite" contains no dialogue and begins with the astronaut's journey to Jupiter, with shots of the monolith making the journey as well. This part of the film resembles a light show, with flashes of pictures and effects, has no narrative to speak of, and feels much like a trippier version of *Fantasia*. The music here is the "Kyrie," *Atmospheres*, and *Aventures*, cut and pasted together by Kubrick, but all composed by Ligeti.

On the Beautiful, Blue Danube, by Johann Strauss Jr. (no relation to Richard), is the other familiar piece in *2001*. Like the final act, the film's first twenty-five minutes, including the first three minutes of blank screen and the entire "Dawn of Man" sequence, have no dialogue. After we've heard Ligeti and the *Zarathustra* introduction (twice), the "Dawn of Man" segment of the movie ends with one of the most famous cuts in cinema as the rest of the film takes place far from Earth. The space shuttle travels to the space station, and Johann Strauss's waltz is heard. At the end of that scene, following a meeting on board the station, *The Blue Danube*, which is a nineteenth-century waltz, named after a river in Europe, is played again as the shuttle travels to the moon. Kubrick uses *The Blue Danube* as traveling-in-space music. The waltz, henceforth stereotyped as "space music" (it was even used in the classic episode of the Simpsons, "Homer in Space"), is reprised a final time during the end credits, the final 4:20 of which is heard over a blank screen.

Kubrick used pre-composed classical music in his films for the rest of his career. He did not completely abandon the use of original music—his daughter, Vivian Kubrick, composed music for *Full Metal Jacket*, as did Jocelyn Pook for his final film, *Eyes Wide Shut*—but *2001* began a stretch where most of the music in his films was taken from the already composed classical repertoire.

He showed off his familiarity with classical music most impressively with the score for *Barry Lyndon*, a film set during the second half of the eighteenth century. Its score incorporates music written during or prior to that period by Mozart, Vivaldi, and Handel—most notably an orchestrated version of a Handel *Sarabande* for harpsichord—as well as folk music, contemporary to the period, much of which has no attributed composer.

Full Metal Jacket is the outlier in the second half of Kubrick's career. Kubrick incorporated a number of pop songs into the film's soundtrack, in addition to an original minimalistic and militaristic score by his daughter, used during the half of the film that is set in boot camp. His decision not to use classical music was not only a departure from his previous four films, but also represented a contrast with two other well-known Vietnam War movies, *Apocalypse Now*, famous in part for its *Ride of The Valkyries* sequence, and *Platoon*, which has Samuel Barber's *Adagio for Strings* throughout.

Following *2001: A Space Odyssey*, Kubrick stayed in the future for his next film, *A Clockwork Orange*. Wendy Carlos contributed a couple of original pieces for *A Clockwork Orange*, as well as electronic renderings of Purcell's *Music for the Funeral of Queen Mary* (the film's "main theme") and Rossini's *William Tell Overture* (the Lone Ranger part). A traditional orchestral recording of Rossini's *La Gazza Ladra* is used throughout the first act, while two of Elgar's *Pomp and Circumstance* marches are used in the second, as is Rimsky-Korsakov's *Scheherazade*, heard while Alex imagines himself in biblical times while reading from the New Testament. And the song "Singin' in the Rain" plays a prominent role.

But the classical music most identified with *A Clockwork Orange* is Beethoven's *Ninth Symphony*, memorable because the music is integral to the film's plot, a device dear to lovers of classical music. In *Apocalypse Now*, for example, as Lieutenant Colonel Kilgore and his subordinates prepare for a raid, they blast Wagner's *Ride of the Valkyries* from giant speakers attached to the outside of their helicopter: "I use Wagner," he explains. "It scares the hell out of the [Vietnamese]."

In *A Clockwork Orange,* after a night of rabble-rousing and ultra-violence, Alex and his three "droogs" end up in the Korova Milk Bar, where a classically trained singer amidst a group of "sophistos" belts out the main vocal melody from the fourth movement of the *Ninth,* the "Ode to Joy." Alex, who doubles as our "humble narrator," is mesmerized. He speaks of his fondness for Beethoven, refers to the composer familiarly as Ludwig van, and violently scolds his fellow droog for making an obscene noise during the singing, the film's inciting incident.

In Anthony Burgess's novel, the piece of music sung in this scene is from a violent moment in the opera *Das Bettzeug,* by Friedrich Gitterfenster. Kubrick was not free to use Gitterfenster's music, though, since both Gitterfenster and his opera are fictional. Burgess similarly fabricated a violin concerto by "Geoffrey Plautus" and a string quartet by "Claudius Birdman," mixed in with brief references to Mozart and Bach, all before Beethoven is even mentioned (Alex visits a record store, wondering if his "long-promised and long-ordered stereo of Beethoven *Number Nine* has come in yet"). In the film, an electronic arrangement of the march from the fourth movement of Beethoven's *Ninth* is used as Alex strolls through the record store.

Alex has a Beethoven poster in his room. Later, while he is shown videos to condition violence out of him, the *Ninth* is played as background music, purely coincidentally, and he screams in objection. The behavioral scientists are surprised to learn that his objection is not to the grotesque imagery on screen, but to the sacrilegious misuse of Beethoven's music. Earlier, one of Alex's victims attempted to defend herself by attacking Alex with a bust of Beethoven, foreshadowing the attack on Alex with Beethoven's actual music. In Burgess's novel, the music heard during the conditioning scene is *Symphony Number Three* by the fictional Danish composer, "Otto Skadelig."

Although *2001: A Space Odyssey* and *A Clockwork Orange* are considered among the greatest of all time, they never achieved the enduring popularity of films like *Indiana Jones*, *Star Wars*, and *It's a Wonderful Life*. *2001* has a reputation as a slow film, one in which nothing happens. *A Clockwork Orange* has a reputation for being controversial (famously banned in the UK for a time), ultra-violent (a phrase coined by the book's author and used in the film), and disturbing (rightly so).

For many film afficionados, the themes of Beethoven's *Ninth* will often bring back scenes from Kubrick's film. But while the beginning of *Also Sprach Zarathustra*, the tone poem, is now almost always associated with *2001*, a parody of *2001*, or science fiction in general, Beethoven's *Ninth* is not as closely linked with *Clockwork*. *Clockwork's* initial X-rating, which limited younger moviegoers and scared off others (*2001* was given a PG-rating), partially explains this. But a bigger factor is surely that Beethoven is a household name, a better-known composer than Richard Strauss, and that the *Ninth* may be his masterpiece. *Also Sprach Zarathustra*, though hardly obscure, had been and still is (except for the first minute-forty-five) overshadowed by other Strauss tone poems—*Till Eulenspiegel*, *Ein Heldenleben*, and *Don Juan*—while Beethoven's *Ninth* is one of classical music's "greatest hits."

Classical music will surely continue to play a prominent role in film. Martin Scorsese, who is known for his effective use of pop music in his films, perhaps best followed Kubrick's lead in putting together an entire soundtrack of pre-recorded classical music for his film, *Shutter Island*, including music by Kubrick favorites Ligeti and Penderecki, as well as Mahler (the Mahler *Piano Quartet* is part of the narrative), John Cage, John Adams, and others. The James Bond film *Quantum of Solace* takes place in part during a performance of Puccini's *Tosca*. The music of *The Mikado* is used throughout the underappreciated Chevy Chase and Goldie Hawn farce, *Foul Play*; the climax of the film even takes place during a staged performance. Verdi's *Requiem* is used in Tarantino's *Django Unchained*. Mahler's *Symphony No. 9* and Tchaikovsky's *Symphony No. 5* are incorporated beautifully into the soundtrack of the Oscar-winning *Birdman*. But few filmmakers have used classical music in ways as interesting, as memorable, or as revolutionary as Stanley Kubrick.

Bone Music

Tim Heerdink

Outlawed tune of the common western man   devil's noise
sought out and destroyed   for traditional pieces
boasting Soviet ideology
must be the only thing
running through   your bones.
No, no, no!   I can't   go on
without the sound   of   rock n' roll
coursing its way up   my heart   into my brain.
Take x-ray pictures,   take my ribs;
make a record   and pass it
to a friend, the fellow in the village over.
Let him hear   that there's no holding a man down forever.

SOUNDTRACK TO A MENTAL BREAKDOWN

Tim Heerdink

Enter scene.

A soft beginning with low bass drum
pitter patter like a heart gone metronome
laying the foundation for the rest.

Wait, oh, there's the bassist
also low in tone but building
with its steady rhythm.

Calm, be quiet.

You don't want to miss
the wakening of guitars,
keys alongside keeping up.

This is nice;
I could be here
for a while.

Such harmo-

Trumpets roaring in an attempt

to outdo the crash of cymbals
skipping any crescendo
now forté.

I'm surely awake
if I wasn't already before.

The amount of time
it took for my mind to realize
it had but long been lost.

Violins | Violence

Tim Heerdink

How did I get this gift / this curse
to take part in a skeletal quartet
while my brothers & sisters fall
in holes they were forced to dig?

My bow down to the last few hairs,
& I hope the soldiers don't turn on me
when these notes no longer can sing.

Faster I play, faster the death comes.

It comes no matter the piece
with no peace in sight
as I close my eyes,
trying to drown
the sound
of each
gun
shot.

OUR SONG IN AFRICA

Bill Hemminger

*Choral music is not one of life's frills. It's some-
thing that goes to the very heart of our humanity, our
sense of community, and our souls. You express, when
you sing, your soul in song. And when you get together
with a group of other singers, it becomes more than the
sum of the parts. All of those people are pouring out
their hearts and souls. . .which is kind of an emblem for
what we need in this world, when so much of the world
is at odds with itself.*

John Rutter

One of the most terrible deprivations of the Covid 2020
year has been that we cannot get together—to sing. And, as
John Rutter so aptly has put it, singing with others allows those
of us with less-than-operatic voices to be part of what might become a tremendously moving sound—the sound of humans
striving together to make musical beauty. Singing also makes
great use of the human body, so that singing with others is
working with them, too. And, working to create some rhythmic, melodic, beautiful sound thus becomes a spiritual activity,
both profoundly private but public too.

My wife Jill and I have been life-long amateur singers and, when possible, members of choral groups. Jill is a conservatory-trained flutist, and I am an amateur pianist—but we both are musicians. In my several years in Africa, where I worked as Fulbright professor in various universities (I am a specialist in literature and languages), we created two choral groups—the OK Chorale in Antananarivo, Madagascar, and the choir of American School of Yaoundé in Cameroon. Our experiences with the singers were entirely positive, and I am pleased to say that many of the bonds we made with singers in both groups have remained to this day.

Friends and family protested when I said that I would accept the Fulbright position at the University of Madagascar. It was 1988, and our daughter Johanna had just been born. You can imagine the questions: How can you take a new-born to an African country? What kind of food will you be able to eat? *Is* there food? What if she gets sick? Truthfully, I had some trepidation, too, since I had spent several years already in West Africa and knew there were risks.

But I was quite wrong. Madagascar is a beautiful country with wonderful, generous people and, in the capital city, a salubrious climate. Johanna, whom the Malagasy called "Yoda," thrived, and we made friends with all sorts of people. I had been assigned to work at the University of Madagascar, built atop a great hill in Antananarivo, which itself is 4000+ feet above sea level and therefore pleasantly temperate. In the Malagasy highlands we had two crops of strawberries a year, in addition to pineapples, mangos, papayas; mid-summer temperatures were never very high, and the dry season in July and August was chilly enough to warrant wearing a jacket—you get the idea. One of the first things I did as Fulbright Professor of American Culture was to establish a choral group, directed by Jill. Not terribly original, I named our group, "The OK Chorale," perhaps in keeping with my role as über-American. I'm not sure anyone there got the joke.

So Jill and I taught note-reading and basic musical literacy (all pretty western) to my students, who were avid learners. In Malagasy society, everybody sings, and everybody harmonizes. Some of the musical impetus may have come from the efforts in the 19th century of the British Missionary Society, which sent scores of starchy Victorians to teach the locals how to worship Christ (not at all an indigenous concept) and how to sing four-part hymns. Later, the French took over and annexed the entire island, though I'm not sure that the French offered much in terms of music; they spent most of their time squelching local culture. But I know that the desire to sing comes from the very social culture that the Malagasy enjoy, irrespective of religion.

In any case, the OK Chorale regularly came together to sing, sometimes on campus and sometimes in our apartment at the foot of the hill. I had brought some sheet music along, mostly fairly-square settings of spirituals with some other anthem-like ditties. The students sang dutifully and boisterously. We performed in public a couple of times throughout the academic year, and we were noticed.

So that towards the end of that academic year—it was already 1989—we got an invitation to perform in the Madagascar Jazz Festival that would take place on the grounds of a beautiful villa outside the city limits. How could we refuse? In addition, the organizers wanted Jill and me to play flute and piano, and we had Claude Bolling's Suite for Flute and Jazz Piano ready to go. Everyone was excited.

The evening of the performance was perfect. It was the dry season, June, so there would be little chance of rain. The venue was probably that of one ambassador or another: they all had huge estates (quite a contrast with the tiny structures most Malagasy inhabit) with lovely, tended grounds and protective perimeter walls with armed security forces. In much of the world, the haves do not easily coexist with the much more numerous have-nots.

Jill and I played early in the program. I had to hand Yoda over to Fidimalala, one of our singers, while we performed to a sun setting in the west and painting the sky in warm colors. Later, the OK Chorale assembled. We got ready: there were about 20 singers, young women and young men; we took our places on the patio-cum-stage of the Festival. As expected, the students were mature performers—no fear, not even the slightest hesitation. I carried Yoda on my shoulders and joined the group as the sun set and we all sang. We finished our textbook version of "Go Down, Moses," slow and lugubrious, and Jill turned and bowed. But then Haingo quietly stepped in, raised his arms, and began to expand on what we had just sung. Wisely, Jill stepped away, joining me and Yoda. Then the OK

Chorale, working ensemble, improvised a riff on that tune that must have gone on for 10 or so minutes: wild rhythmic tempos, my politely musical singers ripping away on this tune, all of us swaying and singing, Yoda clapping, until Haingo brought us (including two very surprised white folks) to a close. Big applause! Imaginary newspaper headline: "The OK Chorale finishes off Madagascar Jazz Festival with a bang!" And here's a lesson for teachers: never underestimate what your students may already know.

Years later I accepted a similar Fulbright position at the University of Cameroon in that country's capital city, Yaoundé. By this time, however, Yoda was 16, and a second daughter, Mollie (who was conceived in Madagascar and whose middle name Nirina, in Malagasy, means "beloved") extended our family group. For the year we were there, both girls attended the private American School Of Yaoundé (known casually as ASOY), one of many such institutions that function in most world capitals as schools for expatriates and their kids. The school employed teachers from all continents, and the student body reflected the typical diversity of embassy and multi-national communities. To add an American to the list, Jill was hired as instructor of the instrumental music program.

And like Antananarivo, Cameroon's capital city was platted (in this case by the Germans) high on a tropical plateau, in an effort to remove sensitive colonial populations from the dangers of malaria in the drenched coastal regions. The original town was conceived on the site of a trading post, where Europeans came to get cocoa, rubber, sugar cane and all the other fruits of an equatorial climate. The city, built on a string of hills and at the verge of the great tropical forests to the south, consists of a series of roadways that corkscrew their way up the hills. ASOY sits atop one of those hills. Of course, that carefully-conceived city map anticipated a total population of, maybe, some tens of thousands of people. When we lived in Yaoundé that number was at least 2.5 million, many people having left the relative poverty of their bush villages to find work in the western-style city. And the original quaint cobbled streets had become over-run with dogs, donkeys, chickens, vehicles in various states of (dis)repair, and the offal (mostly plastic) of all those humans crammed together in a small, constantly warm space.

Jill and I were at it again: we wanted to put together a singing group. Our group took on the *de facto* name of ASOY Choir. We gathered together various members of the ASOY community—a primary school teacher from the West Indies, a high school student (and her mom) from Peru, a physician from Spain, the math teacher (German), several American missionaries and their kids, a few of the African students at ASOY, among others. We met weekly after school hours in the music room that overlooked the school swimming pool (star fruit and lychee trees provided shade). Most students at ASOY, like our own kids, would spend only a year or two before Mom or Dad would be posted somewhere else in the world, and the constituency of the school would change again. Which meant that the end of the school year would be, for many people, a goodbye to friends.

So Jill and I conceived of a valedictory ASOY Choir program. Actually it would be a recital of everything the choir had worked on, but we knew it would all have special significance for many of us. At my insistence we sang one of my favorite compositions by John Rutter, "The Gaelic Blessing," which, with its many references to the balm of the natural world, felt fitting for us as a tribute to the fantastical tropical world we lived in at that time. Last on the program was a piece I composed for our choir, a sort of hymn to the vitality of the city of Yaoundé. The four-part composition consists mostly of vocalized chords that change randomly but which build up to a section where audience members are invited to shout out names of city neighborhoods they know, names that appear on no map but which are known to hard-core residents and are the *de facto* human map of the city. I alerted the audience that they would be involved in the production of this choral work, that they could consider themselves part of the choir (if they wanted) by speaking out the neighborhoods whose names they knew (and which reflect some of the dozens of Cameroonian languages). The ASOY Choir moved deftly through the composition, and at the proper time, I turned to the audience. The response was almost deafening, so many names were fervently proclaimed. Someone said "Bastos," the neighborhood Jill and I and our girls lived in; someone else yelled "Tam-tam weekend" (you can imagine what happens there). Then a proliferation of neighborhood names—Mvolye, Mvog-Beti, Golf, Mokolo, Mbog-

Abang, Mont Fébé—before I waved my hands to close the public participation, and the Choir ended the program. It was our tribute to the vibrant town created by colonials but then taken over by Africans, who made it their own rather noisy super-village. Our song was a big hit.

Jill and I were part of other musical events while we lived in Africa. As instrumentalists, she and I opened the Lobster Festival (actually *langoustes*, small lobsters but equally delicious) in Fort-Dauphin, Madagascar; the upright piano I played on had been hauled in on the back of a pick-up truck from 100 miles away just for the occasion and had suffered greatly from the ride. But that sad instrument allowed me to play one of the national dance tunes in 15/8 time as the Malagasy danced. We also entertained residents of a monastery in Morondava, on the other side of the island, while young men circled the cinder block concert venue pushing away little kids who kept gathering at the open windows. In Cameroon, *we* were treated to a drumming/dancing celebration at the home of one of my university colleagues, all four of us entreated to join the dance line, which we did to the great pleasure of our host. Music is indeed a universal language; music that inspirits social interaction can be a human gift.

But it is choral singing, somehow, that is most precious to me. The "Gaelic Blessing" contains the words "Deep peace of the flowing air to you// Deep peace of the quiet earth to you," and while our feet are planted on the earth as we sing, so too do we form the air into sounds with pitch and with syllables. Of course the "Gaelic Blessing" concludes with a very Christian message, but I think that music transcends all religions. Our experiences in Africa showed us how music can bring people together, despite—or perhaps because of—social, linguistic, religious, and cultural differences. Johanna, Mollie, Jill and I enjoyed all of our African musical experiences, and those experiences remind us all of the people and places we so much grew to love.

ADVENTURES OF A MIDWESTERNER IN IRISH MUSIC

Tom Drury

"Tommy, can you see O'Ryan's belt?"

"Where?"

"Right there! Do you see those three bright stars right in a row like that?"

It's hard to see constellations when you're a little kid. All the stars look the same, and trying to work out how grownups can see things like dragons or hunters can be pretty baffling. But this time I could see right where my father was pointing, and there were three brilliant stars perfectly lined up together.

"Yeah Dad, I see 'em."

"That's O'Ryan's belt!"

The small town in Illinois I grew up in had five thousand people, one stoplight, and two Roman Catholic churches. The Protestants had churches too, of course; there was a Methodist church, a Lutheran church, and another called The Federated Church where Presbyterians and Baptists attended worship together, sang hymns, and listened to the same sermon. The parishioners at the two Catholic churches listened to the same sermon every week, since they shared a priest, but they didn't listen together, and I doubt that they shared much else. St. Joseph's Catholic Church, named for the patron saint of Germany, was attended by families with names like Bloome or Rosentreter. But the people who went to St. Mary's had names like Ryan or Costello. Or Drury. Mary isn't the patron saint of Ireland; that's Patrick, or Paddy for short, from the Gaelic *Padraig.* We had corned beef and cabbage in his honor every year on March 17. But Mary is important enough to Irish culture that Irish Gaelic speakers invoke her when they say hello. Roughly translated, *Dia dhuit* means "God be with you" to which the reply is *Dia is Muire dhuit,* "God and Mary be with you."

I should clear one thing up, if it isn't clear already. There are English Drurys, and there are Irish Drurys. We are Irish Drurys.

I have been told that my versatility is my greatest strength. I think it's at least as likely that my greatest weakness is my inability to stay focused on any one thing long enough to get really good at it. Either way, I've always maintained a wide variety of musical interests. As a young child, I took piano lessons with a local teacher and participated in the distinctly Japanese-flavored Suzuki violin program. The Suzuki teaching method is linguistically conceived, with the idea that children learn music the way they learn to talk, by listening and repeating. I liked learning by listening, but the Suzuki method didn't turn out to be any less restrictive than the please-play-exactly-these-notes-and-no-others way I was taught piano. Whether I was reading notes or learning by listening, I was easily bored and uninterested in playing anything the same way more than once. I liked making up my own stuff to add to whatever I learned, which drew me to jazz in my early teens, once I learned what it was. But I didn't spend much time with non-classical styles of violin playing, and when I did, I played from arrangements of old-time fiddle music in books and didn't really grasp the freedom that style of music entails. Violin playing, as I understood it, meant playing in large groups with other people, everybody playing exactly the same way every time, right down to making sure everyone's bow was moving in the same direction. This required a level of conformity to the group that my teenage self was simply not interested in.

The pipe organ, on the other hand, which I also discovered in my early teens, requires no conforming to any group, and makes an awesome noise. It also happens to be the only instrument in the classical tradition to retain a vibrant tradition in improvisation. So I enrolled as an organ major at the University of Iowa with an additional emphasis in jazz piano. (It took an embarrassingly long time to figure out that I should not say "organ performance" at parties to girls asking what my major was.) Five years later I completed my degree in piano performance and enrolled in the collaborative piano program at the University of Michigan. While I now consider jazz piano to be my primary medium, I never did finish the jazz emphasis.

After completing my MM at Michigan, and after a brief stint with Kentucky Opera where I met my future wife and

learned that I didn't want to work in opera, I found myself waiting tables at a chain Tex-Mex restaurant on the outskirts of Louisville wondering if I should join the Peace Corps. Maybe I'll get
back into church music instead, I thought. I'd given up on not
being a Christian, and the pipe organ really does make an awesome noise, so I called Rudy Zuiderveld, organ professor at Illinois College and my teacher in high school, to ask if there was
anyone near Louisville I could study organ with. He referred
me to his old Michigan classmate, Doug Reed, who was professor of organ at the University of Evansville, who in turn referred
me to a Lutheran church in Evansville that was looking for a full-
time music person who could play the organ, direct the choir,
and lead the praise band. ("Dad, I don't know if I'm qualified to
direct their choir." "Son, why don't you let them decide that?")
And in just the time it took to get from Ash Wednesday to
Easter, I had a long-term full-time music job in about the least
likely place imaginable, at least to me.

Andrea and I got married in July, and in September I made
what at the time seemed a relatively inconsequential decision to
take a part-time position as accompanist for the flagship chorus
of the University of Southern Indiana. Rehearsals were two
hours a day, four days a week, seven months out of the year; my
work there existed as a distant afterthought of my day-to-day
existence as Church Music Guy. But I discovered a lot of great
choral repertoire, which was great, because I was now a choral
director. I had joined the ACDA—American Choral Directors
Association—and in January of 2006, I attended a regional

ACDA conference in Chicago with Daniel Craig, director of choirs at USI.

Dan and I had already discovered a shared interest in what is called "world music," a silly term, in my opinion, since all music made by all people exists in the world, unless somebody out there ever plays that recording we sent out with Voyager 2. Classical ragas from India have little in common with mariachi music from Mexico, and neither of those musics have much in common with the Irish music Dan and I were listening to in his pickup truck on the way to Chicago. He was telling me that we were going to skip the opening ceremonies of the conference in favor of driving down to Joliet for something called a "session". That's when people get together and play Irish music and drink beer, he explained. This sounded fun, so after we checked into the hotel, we got back in his truck and took I-55 to Joliet.

The session was at a very typical Irish-style pub, similar to any number of such establishments in the United States. Ann Arbor and Louisville both have Irish pubs, and they were favorite places of mine during my time in those cities. But I had never been to either while live music was playing. And this was a live music performance unlike any I'd ever witnessed. There was no stage, just ten or twelve people sitting around a big table with musical instruments and, sure enough, in most cases, pints of beer, playing the Irish dance music that goes a mile a minute and never seems to come to a stopping point until all of a sudden it does. And when the music would stop, the people would engage in conversation, sometimes talking for five or ten minutes before resuming the music. There were fiddles and wooden flutes that looked like period instruments they sometimes play Mozart and Beethoven on (which, it turned out, was exactly what they were); a button accordion, the kind that looks like a typewriter; a banjo; a guitar; and somebody with a drum called a *bodhrán* that can be pronounced a few different ways, none of which could be guessed by an English speaker from the spelling. Dan had brought one, too, as well as a couple of tinwhistles. This last is a simple little instrument like a primitive recorder with six holes and several names: tinwhistle, though they're not made of tin anymore; pennywhistle, though even the cheapest cost a few hundred pennies; or just whistle, as if there aren't a million other things also called "whistle". The wildest part was that we sat at the table with them, and Dan played his *bodhrán* and his tinwhistle, even though he had never met any of them before. "Anybody can play if they understand the style," he explained. Yeah? Waitress? Could you bring me two soup spoons, please?

It's more than a little embarrassing in retrospect to remember inserting myself into the performance like that. But the folks were kind and welcoming, and they sold me a CD, and in April, when we got our tax refund, I bought a $600 Hohner piano accordion. Piano accordions have a piano-style keyboard for the right hand and rows of buttons for the left, while button accordions have buttons for both hands. They sound similar, but are played *very* differently, and being able to play one does not in the least mean you'd be able to play the other. My violin had been stolen several years before, and it made more sense in my mind to try something similar to a piano or an organ.

Dan had a group who played Irish music, and I began coming to their rehearsals. They met in a coffee shop once a week and played the tunes. Most of the members brought music stands and played from sheet music, something the folks in Joliet hadn't done. This was comforting. "There's no way I'd be able to memorize all these tunes," I said to Dan one evening.

"If I asked you to sit down and play "A Mighty Fortress Is Our God" without music, would you be able to do it?"

"Well sure."

"It's the same."

I was skeptical.

"I heard you can play accordion."

The personnel manager for the Evansville Philharmonic Orchestra, Tim Smith, was calling. We'd attended a few EPO concerts, and Andrea had sung the soprano solo for their Messiah one December. Tim was wondering if I would be available to play accordion with the EPO for an upcoming pops concert. I thought he was joking. Tim's personality was one where you could never be quite sure if he's being serious. But he was serious. It hadn't crossed my mind that it would be possible to make money playing the accordion when I bought it, and for it to be my first engagement with a professional orchestra, well, "unexpected" doesn't quite cover it. But I took the gig. It's been awhile, and I only now remember two numbers that were on the program: the classic love theme from *The Godfather*, complete with accordion solo, which was why I had been called, and also the iconic, if sappy, love theme from *Titanic*, "My Heart Will Go On;" Hilary Abigana played the flute solo on a keyless wooden flute, the kind of flute I described above that Irish music is traditionally played on. I didn't know anybody else in Evansville played Irish music.

"So you've never been to the session?"

"There's a session? In Evansville?"

"Thursday nights. You should come."

It was a few years before I was able to carve out time for that weeknight slot. Babies don't leave much time for hobbies, and we had two in three years. But by then I had a fiddle, loaned to me by my sister when she didn't want to take it with her to France. Jigs and reels had always felt awkward on my accordion, and only after getting hold of a fiddle again did I realize the tunes aren't designed for a piano accordion. It's fiddle and pipe music. Concertinas and button accordions work well, too, but playing those tunes on a piano accordion is a little like trying to play a violin concerto on a tuba. A really good player can make it work, but they lie under the fingers so much more comfortably on an instrument they're made for.

This session was like most sessions; no music stands allowed. I was starting to realize the extent of freedom allowed, even encouraged. A player of Irish music is expected to ornament, elaborate, and vary the notes of the tune, in direct contrast to classical music in which the performer is expected to play every note that appears in the score. I was also learning that tunes are easier to put in your head if you don't have to remember every note, and that the tradition allows for different musicians to ornament in different ways while playing the same tune together. All this together makes Irish music largely devoid of the pressure that I'd always felt playing classical music—to play perfectly. I shook off the please-play-exactly-these-notes mentality and dove in.

One of the most remarkable things about the traditional Irish music scene is its international character. Sessions take place all over the world, and many of the same tunes are played everywhere. "All over the world" isn't limited to the Irish diaspora, either. Certainly there are sessions in London and Glasgow and Boston and Toronto and Sydney, but there are also sessions in Latin America, Japan, and all over continental Europe—on every single one of my six visits to Ireland I've run into at least one French speaker at a session. Once I attended a session at an Irish pub in Poznań, Poland, where another musician sighed when I said I had Irish ancestry. She wished she did, too, she said. How very strange, I thought but didn't say; every Polish-American I've ever known is fiercely proud of being Polish. Not everyone at that session spoke English, but we mostly knew the same tunes.

Most of the sessions that I've attended outside Evansville have been in Ireland, where USI's mixed choir frequently tours; that inconsequential decision had turned into a full-time teaching position I've held for a decade now. The session experience in Ireland can be somewhat touristy at times. On the west coast, especially, the tiny pubs can overflow with people from Germany to China there to hear the music. These tourists are often surprised to hear my accent, though I'm rarely the only one present who isn't Irish. It's important to note here that the tourist industry isn't just for those who listen to the tunes; every time I go I meet people who regularly travel to Ireland for the express purpose of playing music in pubs, and from as far away as New Zealand. "O'Ryan's" belt is in the northern skies there, and "O'Ryan" is standing on his head.

Once, in Dingle, I walked into a pub that had the words "Irish Session" on the chalkboard out front. Dingle is in the far southwest of the island, near the Ring of Kerry, and it's known for its music and the fact that it is in a *Gaeltacht*, meaning a part of Ireland where Irish Gaelic is still spoken as a first language by a significant percentage of the population. The pub was typically small and cramped, with a few tables and a bar offering the same taps every pub in Ireland offers: Guinness, Bulmer's hard cider, and Budweiser. I had just arrived and was waiting to order a Guinness at the bar before approaching the musicians when the door opened and three young women—maybe early twenties—walked in. They were young, dressed for a night of clubbing, and noticeably intoxicated. They didn't go to the bar, but disappeared toward the back of the pub. I ordered my Guinness, the barman poured it, and while I was waiting for it to settle—the settling of a pint of Guinness is a process taken very seriously in Ireland—two more women, similarly attired, came in and followed the first three. When the musicians finished their tune, I approached them and discovered for the first time that sometimes publicans advertise sessions when they really just mean "live music." But the musicians were kind and welcoming, invited me to sit in, sold me a CD, and asked for an American tune, which I obliged by playing one of the tunes I learned from a book in the third grade. Halfway through "The Devil's Dream", two more women and one young man came in and disappeared similarly into the back. After playing tunes for half an hour and observing every three minutes more young women and an occasional young man continuing to come in the front and disappearing into the back—without returning—my curiosity finally got the better of me.

"These are the future primary schoolteachers of Ireland," the fiddler explained. "The government mandates that the Irish language be taught in the schools, so everyone studying to be a teacher is required to spend a six-week term in a *Gaeltacht*. They have programs here in Kerry, and in Connemara, and up in Donegal... and these just took their exams today. There's a room in the back where they're having a party. They all go home tomorrow."

Ah! That made sense. I found out a few minutes later, when a couple of them, in their high heels and miniskirts, stopped by for a wobbly jig on their way past, that they also learn about traditional Irish culture, music, dance, etc.

The parade continued for the two hours that we played tunes, and when we were done playing, I asked my new friend where the men's room was located, since I had a mile walk back to the room where I was staying. "Back there. Follow those two that just came in." I picked my fiddle up, and he said "Wait. Leave your fiddle here." What? "Trust me. I'll watch it." Ok... I went to the back of the pub where there was a little hallway that went around a corner, then another corner, and then came out into a large room...

Have you ever been to a popular bar in a college town? When I was an undergrad we called that kind of bar a "meat market." This was like that. The mystery of where the young people were disappearing to was solved. "Summer Nights" from *Grease* was being blasted at deafening volume, with hundreds of just-out-of-their-teens Irish people drunkenly screaming along. Flashing disco-style strobe lights completed the experience. The fiddler was right; my fiddle would have been a liability. The joint was so crowded it took five minutes to walk fifty feet, pushing future schoolteachers out of the way the whole time. It was surreal, like I'd been suddenly transported across an ocean and fifteen years back in time to the Union bar on College Street in Iowa City. I understood in that moment why people around the world complain that American culture is taking over everyone else's traditions.

———

It's almost time to go home. I'm sitting in a pub on the north shore of the Liffey in the heart of Dublin, near the bronze Famine statues perpetually staggering east towards the mouth of the river to take ship and leave Ireland forever. Maybe one of them will end up in Massachusetts. Grandpa's people came from Massachusetts to Kentucky before his grandfather came north to Illinois. It's the last night of the tour, and the students have been given the evening free. I've gone off by myself with the emotions that always come with a visit to that country. I'm American, not Irish, and, in addition to the Emerald Isle, the Netherlands, Germany, Scotland, England, and possibly Abraham himself have all contributed to my genetic makeup. But Americans are fascinated with their "roots", and I am no exception. Coming to Ireland always makes me feel somehow closer to where I belong. It isn't home, of course, but always somehow more homelike than home, like a grandparents' house.

A gentleman about the age of my Dutch-American maternal grandfather sits down next to me. Lovely evening, isn't it? It is, it is. Are you from Dublin, sir?

"I am", he replies, "but you're not!"

It's true; just like when I visit my in-laws in Texas, it only takes a couple of words to announce to all within earshot that I'm not from around here.

"My name's Paddy O'Ryan," he tells me. "And you are?"

"Tom Drury," I answer, "nice to meet you."

"*Oh*," he says, eyes lighting up. "You're *Irish*-American!" He beams. "Can I buy you a pint, Tom?

RIVER STREET BLUES

John Guzlowski

In the gray shadows of morning, blues
comes up River Street like a pack of dogs
ready to set you straight if you ain't,
set you right if you're white, the blues

comes up River like a greyhound bus,
packed with 42 tons of Gary steel—
heading for Miami or Atlanta—
that will fuck you up so bad that not all

the mothers in heaven will have enough
tears to soak the sorrow from your eyes
if you get in the way of that north bound,
south bound bus heading out of this town.

These River Street Blues know a thing or two.
They know you got to hold on, hold on to
the night as long as you can 'cause the night
is dreaming. It's a quiet bed loved flat

by dreaming, and not the kind of dreaming
that ends you up in sweat and sticky sheets
but the kind of dreaming that's hungry
for oats and black bread, food you chew

longer than you know how. Food a man wants.
Dreams a man wants. Dreams a woman wants.
Dreams only a child dreams because a child
cannot yet know the truth about dreams,

how they get mixed up and licked up
how they get spewed out and shooed out,
how they grow old and raggedy, fingered
till the colors of me and you both bleed out

and all that's left of the dreams and the child
dreaming them is the thin soup of hope
an old man living alone stores in cans
and stirs in a closet nobody ever sees.

These River Street Blues are a quiet street
of shacks built so long ago there ain't no
granny who can tell you what the door
was colored when it first took a knock.

Hear that knock? It's the River Street blues—
coming to tell you the world needs blues,
needs them like a baby needs candy,
like a woman needs a quick hot spring,

like a man needs the things that keep him
smiling even when the things that keep him
smiling have been gone for so damn long
that nothing is shaking but shaking.

Songs My Father Taught Me

John William McMullen

I was four years old, sitting in my father's lap, and we were listening to music.

"Daddy, why do people sing?"

"Because of Easter."

At the time his answer was more cryptic than helpful, but I never forgot his answer.

———

I grew with music. I can still see my father lifting the lid of the phonograph, as he did countless times, placing a record on the turntable, and, carefully, lowering the stylus onto the vinyl. Taking a seat at his desk he would light a cigarette and, exhaling smoke, lean forward in his chair to examine a spreadsheet, scribbling numbers, and shuffling papers.

From the stereo I heard the chanting monks of Gethsemani Abbey. Prokofiev's *Peter and the Wolf.* Orchestral masterworks across the classical spectrum. Plus Scott Joplin and Herb Alpert and the Tijuana Brass. Glenn Miller, Roger Miller, Sinatra, Elvis, The Carpenters, and The Bee Gees.

And there was Bach. I did not yet know him by name. But I had heard him on our stereo in Pavarotti's performance of

Gounod's *Ave Maria* (based on *Prelude No 1 in C major, BWV 846*). And, though I did not know the music to be Bach's, I had heard it flowing from the pipes at church.

The pipe organ was king of music at the Old Cathedral in Vincennes, Indiana; magnificent, mysterious, compelling. Invisible to my eye, the music entered my ears and took its place in my heart. The pipes never moved, but their sonorous melodies were undeniable. And, for this boy, the louder the better. Whether sitting in the pew or kneeling upon a prie-dieu, I could feel the sound as much as hear it—sometimes feeling the approaching toccata and fugue well before the audible notes ever filled the church.

My fascination with the pipe organ had me walking or riding my bike to Mass early to hear the organist practice. When he played the organ, he became one with the instrument. He was a captain at the helm, commanding rows of keyboards and exerting mastery over a boggling array of stops, levers, and floor pedals. To watch him play was to witness a man in a full-body workout, a highly physical production that rendered cascading melodies, like a waterfall of harmonious vibrations, shaking the church and immersing me in the waves of melody. When the music stopped, the sound reverberated, echoing into a pulsating silence all its own.

All the music I had heard prior seemed so much straw compared to the glory revealed by the pipes. As I knelt in adoration, I had discovered a mystical union; God and music, together. Power and beauty. Might and majesty. Love and its audible expression. The tone, tenor, and timbre of the instrument were beyond words, beyond what my teenage mind could fathom. I stood with Isaiah, finding himself in the Lord's presence as the Seraphim cried out: *"'Holy, Holy, Holy'* . . . *and the foundations shook and the house was filled with smoke"* (Is. 6:3-4); I was with the Apostles when, after praying, *". . . the place where they had gathered shook and they were all filled with the Holy Spirit"* (Acts 4:31).

I had tasted musical grandeur and I longed for more. The voice of this august instrument penetrated me, reaching the depth where heart and soul meet. For many of my friends, and not a few parishioners, the instrument evoked dark feelings, even gothic horrors—Dracula and Frankenstein, haunted mansions. But the ethereal breath of these pipes inspired a spirit of fervor within my inmost being, bearing the joy of salvation.

When I at last introduced myself to the organist, he shared the names of favored composers: J.S. Bach, Louis Vierne, Charles Marie-Widor, Marcel Dupré, Maurice Duruflé, and Olivier Messiaen, among others. I soon discovered public radio and university stations were rich avenues for listening. *Pipedreams,* hosted by noted organist and organ scholar Michael Barone, took me on wonderful adventures through the pipe organ repertoire.

Bach's influence upon my life continued beyond high school and into college, when I came to a pivotal moment in my musical education. In the spring of 1985, while a student at Vincennes University, my philosophy professor, Dr. Bernard

Verkamp, offered me a complimentary ticket to a concert celebrating the 300th birthday of Bach. It featured the Baroque orchestra and choral singers from Indiana University led by distinguished professors Stanley Ritchie, violinist, and Thomas Binkley, lutenist.

For reasons I don't recall, I almost didn't go. But I'm glad I did. The experience changed my life.

The moment I heard the original Baroque instruments and voices sing forth was an apocalypse in the truest sense of the word—unveiling a sonic world that allowed me to hear music as if for the very first time. As the organ pipes conveyed the breath of God, the keyboards, strings, woodwinds, and horns combined with human voices transported me to a place of indescribable beauty.

I have long since lost the program notes for that evening, but some of the selections likely included *Preludio from Violin Partita No.3 in E major*; choral works of *Sleepers, Awake*; *Jesu, Joy of Man's Desiring*; *Sheep May Safely Graze*; *Magnificat*; works from the *Anna Magdalena Notebook*; selections from the *Brandenburg Concertos*; the sublime prayer *Erbarme dich,* from the *St. Matthew Passion;* and the *Agnus Dei* from his *Mass in B minor.*

On that spring night, the musical legacy of Johann Sebastian Bach awakened me to a whole new world, bridging three centuries between a philosophy student and one of the greatest composers of all time.

Beethoven said: "His name should not be Bach [Brook], but Mer [the Sea]." Mozart's tribute is equally praiseworthy: "He is the Father, we are his Children."

Bach is indeed the ocean and we all swim in his music.

———

In the last years of my father's life, I reminded him of our exchange about why people sing, but he neither recalled my question nor his response.

Whether my father knew it or not, when he answered my question, he echoed the sentiments of J.S. Bach, who wrote: "The aim and purpose of all music should be for the Glory of God and the recreation of the human spirit."

Indiana writer Kurt Vonnegut wrote, "Let this be my epitaph: the only proof he needed for the existence of God was music."

Bach proved to me that music does exist.

That sounds a lot like Easter to me.

BACH TO THE FUTURE

John Siau

Perhaps my most vivid memory from fourth grade at Harper School was failing a music pitch and rhythm test.

The principal came on the public address system and informed us that we were to listen to a series of musical tones, decide which was highest and which was lowest, then record our answers on a scoresheet our teacher, Mrs. Trabits, had distributed as we entered the room. I recorded my choices and felt good about my effort. Mrs. Trabits collected the answer sheets and then we continued with our regularly scheduled assignment.

Several weeks went by before we heard the results of our foray into the wonderful world of music. Sitting atop the teacher's desk one day was a large cardboard box, and we anxiously awaited the revelation as to its contents. Then Mrs. Trabits reached inside and began removing smaller boxes as our imaginations ran wild. As she unloaded all the smaller boxes, she told us that we were receiving tonettes. What's a tonette I pondered? Mrs. Trabits opened one of the small boxes to reveal a black plastic song flute.

Touring the room row by row, Mrs. Trabits informed the class that, based on our musical tone test, we would be receiving one of the fascinating instruments. Methodically, she began handing them out. She was getting closer: Maidlow, Majors, Meier, Ogg, Overton, Padgett, Pyle, Shoulders, Singleton . . . Singleton? Wait a minute. Siau comes before Singleton! As my classmates began experimenting with their tonettes, I sat in my seat wondering why I had been passed by. After distributing the last song flute to my excited classmates, Mrs. Trabits motioned for me to come to her desk at the front of the room. Quietly she whispered in my ear that I had miserably failed my test. In fact, I got a zero.

That evening as I lay on my bed sulking, my father knocked gently on my bedroom door and then entered. He had noticed during supper that I was upset about something and thought it best to see what was bothering me. We sat on the edge of my bed and I began recounting the events of the day. My father listened as I revealed that I had failed miserably. Suddenly, my father began to smile. Oh great, now my own father found my failure funny. His hand tousled my hair as he said, "Join the club, son." This only added to my bewilderment. Then he began telling me of the family curse. A curse that went back as far as anyone could ever remember. No one on his side of the family tree or my mother's side had any pronounced musical talent whatsoever.

Legend holds that perhaps someone deep in our ancestral history had been blessed with ALL of our family's allotted musical talent.

After my classmates had practiced for several months, it was time for their musical debut with the Evansville All-City Band and Orchestra. They would be boarding buses for their trip down Division Street to Roberts Municipal Stadium, where they would join seemingly every other kid in Evansville for the musical concert of the year. I, on the other hand, would spend the three and a half hours of isolation in Mrs. Trabits's room.

As I watched my friends file past me one by one, I seemed to be melting into my seat. Finally, as I saw Harold Jensen and David Woods turn to mock me, I realized I had to make the most of my confinement. Two options came to mind: use the time to study or wile away the hours drawing—DRAWING IT SHALL BE! The only person I saw during that time frame was Mr. Perrin, the school custodian. I can only assume that he had been instructed to check up on the school's only musically-challenged student as his schedule would allow.

I remember that day distinctly. The sky was a cerulean blue with hardly a wisp of a cloud. There was a gentle breeze coming from the windows on the room's north side. Having been at the stadium a billion times, I knew that all of the heavy doors around the building would be propped open to allow air to circulate so that the musicians and patrons could survive the humid spring weather. I began creating one crayon masterpiece after another. I could hear the faint echoes of my more musically gifted friends as they joined in unison to play "This Is Our Story." Later, as my classmates filed back in, they were greeted with some thirty drawings that I had carefully placed around the room. Perhaps I was musically inept; however, darn it, I could draw!

There was yet another occasion where the family curse hexed me. Now in the fifth grade, we began alternating days of art and music. This proved to be an emotional roller coaster for me. When in Mr. Schmidt's art class, I was elated and thirsting for knowledge about all that is art. Yet, the next day was spent in Mrs. Dugger's musical dungeon. No offense to Mrs. Dugger, but my musical failures transferred from instrumental music into vocal music.

Our principal, Mr. Wiseman (yes, that was actually his name), announced that in three weeks the entire school would take part in the annual "Choir Night." Darn my luck! Surely, knowing my utter failure on the previous pitch and rhythm test, the teachers would allow me to hone my artistic skills rather than subject me to further humiliation.

Our class was chosen to sing "God Bless America." Mrs. Dugger handed us our sheet music to study. She had taught us to read the music, however, I had seen no reason to listen since I was not going to be a musician. Daily, she would take pieces of chalk and embed them into a curious-looking device with wire extensions mounted on a wooden handle. Then she would press the device against the chalkboard and make perfectly spaced lines on which she would put a series of ovals with curious lines extending upward. I found the chalk device fascinating, but the odd-looking "notes" (as she called them) appeared to me as alien as one could ever imagine.

As the "Choir Night" approached, Mrs. Dugger decided to ascertain who the soloist would be, so she announced that each student would, in alphabetical order, approach the front of the room and sing the first three lines of "God Bless America." Panic, then horror, beset me.

The first to try out was my dear friend Rawson Atkin, a boy with significant "pipes." As he sang, others responded by nodding in affirmation. The kid could sing! I was proud of my buddy. Then in succession, other classmates took their turn. Mrs. Dugger smiled as one after the other impressed her. Again the order was alphabetical and I was running out of time. I had heard myself sing; it was not a pleasant experience. Plus there was the family curse. Fate was about to rear its ugly head once more. I prayed that Mr. Wiseman would suddenly break in with an impromptu civil defense drill. You know . . . assume the position—drop and cover under your desk and remain quiet until further notified." But, alas, no such announcement was forthcoming.

Time was running out. Mike Shoulders took his stance aside the piano, cleared his throat, and awaited the nod from Mrs. Dugger and a brief tinkling of the ivories. Mike was a good friend, and I had yet to find anything he was less than perfect at. Oh great, once again I got to follow Mike Shoulders. Nervously, I kept hoping for divine intervention, a nuclear attack, anything that would save me from my impending doom. Upon completion, Mike received affirmation from Mrs. Dugger—and all the girls as well.

Gazing through the classroom windows, I saw neither God's loving hands descending from the heavens nor a Russian bomber plane approaching. It became obvious that I was about to embarrass myself once again!

Mrs. Dugger called my name and I reluctantly began my journey toward her upright Baldwin piano. I was hoping for a phone to ring . . . a call from the governor sparing me from this impending cruel and unusual punishment. No such luck! The time had come. I held my sheet music up, raised my chin, and awaited Mrs. Dugger's cue.

Suddenly, I had a flashback to my days at Walnut Street Baptist Church and Reverend Lawrence. Reverend Lawrence would have the young children sit before him on the first pew, across from the deacons. This would hopefully ensure we would pay attention to his lengthy sermons on hell. He would periodically ask the congregation to rise and "make a joyful sound unto the Lord." After a passionate rendition of "The Old Rugged Cross," he stared down on me from the pulpit and said, "Young man, I said make a **JOYFUL** sound unto the Lord!" Even a man of the cloth had found fault with my singing. Was there no mercy to be bestowed on my soul?

As Mrs. Dugger began playing the introduction, I began sweating profusely. She nodded and I began what I thought was singing. The penciled-in eyebrows above Mrs. Dugger's now-bulging eyes seemed to soar to the ceiling as she abruptly ceased her accompaniment. Gathering her composure, she leaned over to me and asked, "Aren't you the kid that likes to draw?"

"Yes," I responded.

Biting her lip and biding her time, she then asked if I watched any television.

Again I replied, "Yes."

After hesitating, she then asked what shows I watched.

I replied, "*The Red Skelton Show* and *The Ed Sullivan Show*."

Where was she going with this line of questioning? Then Mrs. Dugger said that often the French pantomimist, Marcel Marceau, would perform on The Ed Sullivan Show.

"Do you know what that means?"

"Yes, he doesn't talk or make any sounds. He acts with his hands, and he uses facial expressions to tell his story."

"That's what I want you to do from now on. Just act like you are singing. Do you understand?"

I responded quickly with a resounding, "Sure thing! I can do that."

Two weeks later we assembled on a Thursday night to showcase our musical talents in front of our families. Each grade took their turn on stage. I, although one of the shorter choir members, was assigned to stand atop the risers, on the back row. As we began our rendition of "God Bless America," I started employing every arm gesture and facial contortion I could think of. I was acting, not singing. But, was I giving it my best!

After the "Choir Night" concluded, I began my search for my parents. Throngs of people filled the lobby of the auditorium, making my quest difficult. Suddenly, I saw my father's head above the others. My parents seemed engulfed by other parents, so I waited for the other adults to depart. My parents had expressions of confusion on their faces. Kneeling down and placing his right hand on my bony shoulder, my father said how everyone was complimenting them on my outstanding singing ability. Now it was my time to smile and laugh. I told him about my "tryout" and how Mrs. Dugger directed me to "act" like I was singing.

As reality set in that their son was indeed living proof of the age-old family curse, both my father and mother smiled and laughed. Thank God their son could draw. We walked to the exit and began our short trip home to 15 North Spring Street.

Each of us has a talent that separates us from those around us. I was fortunate to discover mine at an early age. Artistic talent, musical talent, and athleticism usually surface at an early age. Our teachers reinforce our understanding of our strengths and make us aware of our weaknesses. Hopefully everyone will realize their talents and unique assets and strive to incorporate them into their professional and private lives. Some talents take years to discover. Understanding your strengths and weaknesses is one of life's greatest lessons.

As for the family curse, let it be known that my father's theory, and that of countless others in our lineage, has been proven. They assumed that, since there was no pronounced musical talent in our family, someone long, long ago must have received the lion's share of our family's musical talent.

Upon retiring, my mother's brother, Dr. Grover Cleveland (G.C.) Miller traced our family tree back to seventeenth-century Germany, where he discovered the answer. On March 21, 1685, in the central German city of Eisenach, one Johann Sebastian Bach was born. Yes, THE Johann Sebastian Bach. It turns out that Bach is my ninth great grandfather. Even I know that he, his siblings, and four of his twenty children were composers. The mystery as to who got all of our family's musical talent had been solved.

As an epilogue, during their migration to Eastern Kentucky in the 1800s, the family changed the pronunciation of its name to "Back." After receiving this information, I visited my parents' gravesites on Evansville's west side. As I looked down at their marker, then as I looked heavenward, I revealed the answer to the age-old family curse. I can picture my parents enjoying a warm embrace and a good laugh.

HOUSES OF WAR

Antonia Matthew

Second Essay for Orchestra, op. 17
Samuel Barber

"The only influence intrinsic to the music that may be discernible,"
remarked Barber, "is the fact that the piece was written in wartime."

I.
these houses have no locks
these houses have no doors
these houses have no rooms

only spaces

where walls and ceilings used to be
where stoves heated porridge and boiled eggs
where bath tubs waited for children
beds welcomed lovers

cellars from which the coal has been stolen
are open to the air
choked with rubble—plaster, bricks
floorboards, splintered glass

where roofs once were
only memories
– children playing in attics
among old trunks and unused furniture

where a lone wall still stands
tattered wall paper, ends of beams
broken window frames, shredded curtains

and over it all, odor of fire

II.
in the garden
herbaceous borders
are smothered in weeds
only foxgloves rise tall

by day, in this wilderness
children roam

the gardens their jungles
the houses their territories
to which they need no key
the remains of gone lives
—fragments of china, glass,
wisps of fabric, a doll's arm
broken building blocks, --
are grabbed, bartered, fought over

these crumbling treacherous ruins
—where feral creatures hide --
are their mountain ranges,
caves, mazes, ancient cities
where battles, deeds of daring are enacted

III.
when dusk comes, the children leave
as the lamplighter rides his bicycle
down the street, lifting his long pole

to light the scattered gas lamps
then, the ruins, the wild gardens
belong to the displaced,
the casualties of war?—homeless
injured, unemployed —
who scavenge for anything of value
—bricks and planks handy weapons
for staking out a corner --
or drink, or have rough, forced sex
or simply find
shelter for the night

IV
before dawn, when the lamplighter returns
to snuff out the lamps
the night people leave

the houses, the gardens, emerge
as if shaking off the night
and wait

for their families to return
daily life resume its familiar routine

RETHINKING STEM, STEAM, AND MUSIC EDUCATION

Dennis Malfatti

A version of this article appeared in the Winter 2019 edition of *ICDA Notations*, the official publication of the Indiana Choral Directors Association. The previously published sections are reprinted here by permission of ICDA.

One can often sense tension whenever the acronym "STEM" comes up in a conversation among music teachers. There's the predictable eye-rolling, the tacit acknowledgement that we're on the same team, a team dedicated to pushing back on the evils of too much emphasis on STEM. No doubt, the narrow emphasis on STEM as the end goal of all educational endeavors hasn't been great for arts education. Nevertheless, when we break STEM down into its constituent parts (science, technology, engineering, and mathematics), a more nuanced picture emerges, one that has implications for music education.

In Ancient Greek thought, a distinction was sometimes made between *epistêmê*, which refers to pure knowledge, independent of its application to daily life, and *technê* which refers to a skill or craft which may be derived from knowledge. Science and math are intellectual pursuits that can stand on their own (*epistêmê*.) Technology and engineering are practical applications of that knowledge (*technê*.) The problem with STEM isn't that it does not make room for the arts. The problem with STEM is that it lumps science, math, technology, and engineering together into a single subject, thereby removing any distinction between *epistêmê* and *technê*. As an acronym, STEM implies that the value of science and mathematics is measured by their utility in spawning technology and engineering. This narrow attitude is wrong and, indirectly, is the real culprit in the tension between music education and STEM education.

The history of science and mathematics has been largely led by brilliant thinkers motivated by nothing more than relentless intellectual curiosity and a passion for knowledge. While many individuals who work in the fields of science and math undoubtedly do so for the practical benefits derived from their disciplines, the greatest scientific minds in history, from Newton, to Einstein, to Schrödinger, were motivated simply by a thirst for discovery. The countless applications of their work, from space shuttles to smart phones, were byproducts that only later emerged. The *epistêmê* drove the *technê* but the pursuit of the former was in no way dependent upon the promise of the latter.

Many of us in the arts are complicit in promoting narrow attitudes about science and math which, paradoxically, only hinders our advocacy for arts education. The effort of some arts educators to change STEM to "STEAM," in which the "A" stands for "art," only exacerbates the problem. Like STEM does to science and mathematics, STEAM commandeers the arts into the ultimate goal of maximizing utility for practical endeavors. STEAM does nothing to further the arts as an independently valuable endeavor. Moreover, we often view science, math, and the arts as caricatures in opposition to each other: science and math are "left-brain, mechanistic, soulless, and ossified;" art and music are "right-brain, creative, soulful, and squishy." Science and math aficionados are often just as guilty of promoting these stereotypes as art and music advocates are.

As an alternative to this simplistic dualism, consider the words of one of the most influential and outspoken biologists of our time, Richard Dawkins, who said in an interview:

> I think there are two main ways of thinking about science. There's the "isn't it wonderful" approach, and then there's what I call the "non-stick frying pan" approach which is, "well, we must support NASA because non-stick frying pans were developed as a byproduct of their work." When I'm asked to justify science education, I do not, as some do, leap first for what is useful. Instead, it's the beauty of the universe, the awe-inspiring nature of the cosmos and the deep complexity in biology [which justifies science education] (Dawkins).

In another context, Dawkins said:

> The usefulness of science is sometimes exaggerated. You'd never talk about music being useful, or art being useful...music is beautiful, music is inspiring. And so is science. I'm of the Carl Sagan school of science writing—it should be beautiful and inspiring and enthralling and thrilling. Because reality is all those things (Brown).

Consider too the words of the theoretical physicist, cosmologist, and best-selling author Lawrence Krauss. In an NPR interview, Krauss was asked what the practicality of studying cosmology and astrophysics is. He responded:

> Well, what does a Bach cantata or a Picasso painting do for us? I think the point is we are human beings, and one of the most wonderful aspect of being human beings is being creative and asking questions and trying to understand our place in the universe. For me, one of the great virtues of science is it's a cultural activity, like art and literature and music. It enhances the experience of being human, and it addresses the questions that I'm sure you've asked about your own existence. And if we can get new insights into our own existence and our place in the cosmos, well, that's what happens when we attend a good play or see a good painting. Now there are always side benefits of doing [science]; when we push the limits of technology, and we develop tools that later on are used in society. But I don't think we should justify this remarkable adventure just because of the side effects (Krauss, 33).

Beauty, awe, creativity, enhancing the experience of being human…these are words not from the mouths of musicians and poets, but from the mouths of a celebrated biologist and a prominent physicist describing what motivates them to be scientists. Far from being our opponents, these scientists are in many ways our kindred spirits.

The parallel aims of mathematics, science, music, and the search for ultimate meaning are as old as the disciplines themselves. In the fifth century BC, the Greek mathematician and philosopher Pythagoras developed a set of ideas that bridged mathematics with harmonic pitch relationships in music. For Pythagoras and his followers, music was the language of mathematical perfection and of metaphysical truth. For them, music was a representation of the structure of the universe. These ideas were more than just intellectual puzzles. Pythagoreanism was infused with a religious fervor. Bertrand Russell wrote that a sense of "ecstatic revelation" was present among those who followed Pythagorean theories (Russell). The Roman statesman Boethius further developed and expanded Pythagorean concepts of music in the sixth century AD. More than a millennium later, the influential 17th century astronomer and mathematician Johannes Kepler continued to hold the view that music mirrored the harmony of the planets and stars (Wolff, 7).

How might we as musicians and arts educators benefit from a point of view that sees science and mathematics as endeavors motivated by the same passion for ennobling the human experience? How might we communicate this shared goal to colleagues in science and mathematics who may view music as just a happy diversion from "real subjects" or to parents who may be doubtful that their child's involvement in music is worth their time and energy?

We can start by not being afraid to embrace the consilience of science, math, and music and to stop worrying that embracing this consilience will somehow diminish the magical quality of music. As the Greeks knew long ago, music is dependent on mathematics and physics. The formation of regulated sound through the human voice or a musical instrument is at its core, basic physics. The relationship of mathematics to consonant pitch relationships as described by Pythagoras formed the justification for music as one of the seven liberal arts. The perfect intonation choirs often seek in unaccompanied music is the aural manifestation of just intonation in which pitches are related by ratios of whole numbers. When we speak of dark tone or bright tone, we are referring to varying amplitudes of sympathetic vibrations across the spectrum of overtones, a concept covered in most introductory physics classes. The arithmetical pattern known as the Fibonacci series can be found throughout music cross culturally. With regards specifically to singing, human anatomy and physiology are fundamental to understanding how the voice works.

When attempting to convince the scientifically minded of the power of music to improve human well-being, rather than resorting to the hackneyed and dubious "music makes you smarter" claim, we might instead explore the burgeoning field of music therapy in which music is used in clinical settings to improve cognitive and motor functions in individuals ranging from children with autism to senior citizens with Alzheimer's.

We might then find contexts in which the science surrounding music can be incorporated into our interactions with students, parents, administrators, and others. One doesn't have to be a science or math whiz to do this. In my own experience as a choral conductor, I sometimes talk to my singers about the basic physics of intonation. While the explanation alone doesn't help them sing better in tune, it does help them realize that perfect intonation is an objective, science-based reality, not the subjective whim of an irritated choir director. In no way does exploring the science behind music rob it of its aesthetic, emotional, and creative elements. Instead, it links what we consider beautiful and meaningful in music to an objective reality.

Musicians and music educators like to claim that music is multidisciplinary. The beauty of this statement is that it is objectively true. The deeper we explore the multidisciplinary qualities of music, and the more we recognize that when at their best, science, mathematics, the humanities, and the arts are all driven by similar goals, the less we might be on the defensive with those whose inclinations are exclusively in science and math.

Works Cited

Dawkins, Richard. "The Poetry of Science: Richard Dawkins and Neil deGrasse Tyson." *Richard Dawkins Foundation for Reason and Science*, October 20, 2010.

Brown, Eryn. "Q&A: Richard Dawkins Discusses Evolution, Religion, and His Fans." *Los Angeles Times*, November 30, 2013.

Krauss, Lawrence. "Lawrence Krauss On 'A University From Nothing,'" *Talk of The Nation, NPR*, January 12, 2012.

Russell, Bertrand. *A History of Western Philosophy*. New York, NY: Simon & Schuster, 1945.

Wolff, Christian. *Johann Sebastian Bach: The Learned Musician*. New York, NY: W.W. Norton, 2000).

THE INFLUENCE OF RELIGION ON CLASSICAL MUSIC

Reverend James Koressel

My life and appreciation of music took a significant right turn in late August of 1957. At the ripe age of 14 my father and mother delivered me into the care of the Benedictine Monks and Brothers of St. Meinrad Archabbey. I entered the Seminary to begin my studies for the Priesthood.

At St. Meinrad, the monks and students gathered several times each day for prayer. It was rare to hold a prayer service without music, and in this instance the music was the centuries-old Gregorian Chant, sung from a huge book of over two thousand pages known as the "Liber Usualis." The Vatican edition of the music was used for worship services in the Catholic Church, compiled by the Benedictine Monks of the Abbey of Saint-Pierre de Solesmes in northern France. Ancient melodies used by the Jews and Greeks became the basis for many of the Chant melodies.

The Seminary provided a huge library of classical music. During my time there, nearly all of the records were of the 78 rpm variety. This library opened up a new and wonderful world to me. Gradually I was introduced and became addicted to the beautiful world of classical music.

My purpose in this brief essay is to show the influence of religion on classical music, and it seems proper to begin with Gregorian Chant inasmuch as classical composers have tapped into this source for inspiration many times. This is particularly true of the "Requiem Mass," which was sung at funerals. The melody of the "Dies Irae," the *Sequence,* shows up in many pieces: Berlioz, *Symphonie fantastique;* Liszt, *Totentanz;* Saint-Saëns, *Danse macabre;* Rachmaninoff, *Rhapsody on a theme by Paganini, The Isle of the Dead, Symphony No. 3,* and *Symphonic Dances.*

The influence of Christian worship on the major composers is clear. Many composed a *Requiem*, or Mass for the Dead. Palestrina, Lassus, Vittoria, Berlioz, Brahms, Britten, Verdi, Mozart, Faure, Cherubini, and Dvorak all composed a *Requiem*, or "Mass for the Dead." Composers wrote settings for the Requiem Mass as early as the 16th Century. However, it was not until the late 18th century that this art form became popular. Even modern composers like John Rutter and Karl Jenkins have given the world outstanding examples of the Requiem Mass.

Classical composers soon after began to produce music for Masses other than Requiems. These were often spectacular works which required huge orchestras and choruses. No Mass equals Beethoven's *Missa Solemnis.* However, Bach's *Mass in B-minor,* at a performance length of more than two hours and written during the 1730s, a hundred years before Beethoven's piece, has the reputation for being one of the great landmarks in music. *The Armed Man: A Mass for Peace,* by Karl Jenkins, provides an entirely new and dynamic experience. Leonard Bernstein also composed a Mass, his for theatrical presentation.

Catholic and Lutheran Masses were not the only inspiration for classical composers. Other parts of the prayer life of the Church served in that capacity. The Divine Office, another official prayer of the Church, contained a great hymn of Thanksgiving at the conclusion of the morning prayer. It gets its title from the first two words of the prayer: "Te Deum." The words of this hymn of thanks inspired many classical composers to create new settings for them.

Other prayer services were inspirational to the world's great composers. In the Catholic tradition, there is a prayer service called *The Way of the Cross*. This consists of fourteen scenes of the last days and hours of the suffering and death of Jesus Christ. Following a brief meditation and prayer at each picture, a brief hymn is sung. It is called the *Stabat Mater* or "The Mother Standing." These short verses reflect what Mary, the Mother of Jesus, and others may have felt as they witnessed this scene. Dvorak, Rossini, Vivaldi, and, in the modern era, Karl Jenkins wrote their versions of this hymn.

Worship and prayer were not the only religious influences on the world of classical music. The words of the Bible led to the composition of some of the most beloved music of all time. Using the words from *Genesis*, Franz Joseph Haydn composed a brilliant oratorio called *The Creation*.

A much more familiar Oratorio was composed by George Frideric Handel. His *Messiah* is perhaps the most performed classical work. It has endured over 250 years of performances and remains a steady favorite. Handel's masterful use of the words of prophets, angels, and other biblical persons portrays the life of Christ from beginning to end. Has anyone in our world not heard and enjoyed the great "Hallelujah Chorus?"

Johann Sebastian Bach was so inspired by the account of the suffering and death of Christ that he composed the *St. Matthew Passion*. It has been said that Bach's artistry and personality rested on his religiousness. For Bach, art was religion. Proof of this is adequately given in this monumental work. Parts of this work still live among us in the form of hymns sung in our churches. "O Sacred Head Surrounded" can be found in most church song books. Bach's musical and lyrical genius ensure that this masterpiece will continue to touch the lives of many.

The events recorded in Scripture inspired additional classical works. The following represent a partial list of such works: Berlioz, *L'enfance du Christ*; Handel, *Saul, Israel in Egypt*; Stravinsky, *Symphony of Psalms, Noah and the Flood, Lamentations of Jeremiah*; Schütz, *Seven Last Words, Psalm of David*; Prokofiev, *Prodigal Son*; Mendelssohn, *Paul, Elijah*; Saint-Saëns, *The Flood, Samson and Delilah*. While some of these are not as widely known, as appreciated, or as frequently performed as *The Messiah* or *The Passion of St. Matthew*, they are nonetheless works that have enriched the world of classical music.

I would be remiss if I failed to mention some popular compositions of a religious nature. The *Ave Maria* of Bach/Gounod along with Schubert's version has become a favorite at weddings and funerals. The beautiful *Sheep May Safely Graze* and *Jesu, Joy of Man's Desiring* both flow from the deep faith of Bach. Mozart's

Ave Verum is a touching presentation of Mary and her Son. The list of faith-inspired music is endless.

In conclusion, I would dare say that the relationship between religion and classical music is more profound than many would imagine. The expression of faith through music has always been and will continue to be an important and beautiful art form.

SUMMER BEATS

Daniel Wright

A world of technicolor
with dancing in the street
Summer windows blast their preferences
Bass heavy cars rattle in rhythm
Tchaikovsky and Mozart
in the DNA from birth
along with twelve-bar blues

Finding your theme
the music that speaks to your soul
more than anything else
means you've got killer walking music
that makes you feel
like Tony Manero

The future is unwritten virtual insanity
Time to find the new religion
Leave the cross
Keep the lessons
Beethoven keeps his ear to the ground
for what's coming up

as the couple who lives above him
dance to sweet love

What's new is old and what's old is new
A song is a tamed mare
while music is a band of wild horses
Triple digit weather is reprieved
by a cool drink and a nice song
Some dance on the ceiling
while others dance on the stairs
and Fred Astaire smiles on them all

Every song a different color
a different shade
Classical waltzes with Metal
Punk pogos with Hip-Hop
Jazz drinks with Folk
Different colors shine brighter
for every person
And some songs shine brightly
for every to love
And as a man passes
another summer window
he hears Billy Joel claim,
"It's still rock n' roll to me"

GIVE ME MILES

Daniel Wright

Give me Miles
warts and all
Give me bebop punk jazz
that tells Duke Ellington
to shove it up his ass
A beat that lingers like a car
going for a joyride in a roundabout
That sees the space to move
where others just go ahead

Give me every great album
with a bad pun for a title
that acts as a middle chapter
between the Milestones
That start like a jet engine
and put me in a trance
where I start hitting the typewriter
like a man possessed
The notes and the clacks ringing out
as though the highway of the mind
is passing by

Give me the veiled insult to Nancy Reagan
who never knew who he was
when he was being honored that night
by her husband
after he explained again and again
who he was
and why he was there
"It's not like I do anything important
like fuck the President."

Give me the lost projects
that exist in another timeline
The failures and the fulfillments
The moments alone
when he had no one to face but himself
Give me every time
a needle hits
the outskirts of a record
when you hear that one pop
before the music starts
Give me all of that
and you shall find a freedom
in one beautiful glimpse

THE SIGNAL NOBODY KNEW THEY WERE WAITING FOR

Carina Wahlstrom

Surely the first signal sent across the airwaves was music to Guglielmo Marconi's ears. His discovery in 1895 launched the fantastically dramatic birth of the radio. Inventors like Lee DeForest, David Sarnoff, and Edwin Armstrong raced to patent their equipment and produce the highest quality of sound that could broadcast the farthest. Corporations like Westinghouse Electric Company, American Telephone & Telegraph, General Electric, and Radio Corporation of America competed over sales. New stations battled over airtime. Eras of music flourished and died because of the radio.

Radio was a free medium to the public and was consensually believed to belong to the people. World War I suspended this right to the radio when President Woodrow Wilson ordered all broadcasters, professional and amateur alike, to go silent to protect the country in 1917. Hobbyists, dubbed "radio enthusiasts," were still able to experiment as many of them were hired to work for the war effort. The United States Navy was already using wireless communication with bases on land, and the war only escalated the advancement of radio for communication, although, homing pigeons remained the primary method for sending messages over the battlefield. Two years later the President lifted the ban, intentionally avoiding further government interference with this invention.

Few saw the commercial and recreational potential of the ability to transmit one signal to thousands of listeners over hundreds of miles. AT&T, for instance, focused on radiotelegraphy with the goal of improving one-on-one communication. Manufacturers relied on sales rather than producing content in order to make a profit. No one believed they had information worth sharing or that anyone would want to listen to it.

Westinghouse was the first major corporation to create something on a large scale. Enthusiasts applied for a license to transmit under the Radio Act of 1912 in order to talk to one another, but no one attempted broadcasting to the masses or scheduling regular shows. Westinghouse launched the first radio station licensed by the US government, KDKA, on November 2, 1920. KDKA made history by announcing the winner of the twenty-ninth presidential election, Warren G. Harding, thus igniting the commercial industry of radio.

The pioneers of radio also had a vision that would push wireless entertainment into society. Lee DeForest, the self-proclaimed "Father of Radio," and David Sarnoff, president of RCA, dreamed of nationwide broadcasting. DeForest sought to carve an "invisible empire of the air" (Burns, *Empire of the Air*). He dreamed of becoming a legacy. "My present task (happy one) is to distribute sweet melody broadcast over the city and sea, so that in time even the mariner far out across the silent waves may hear the music of his homeland" (Douglas 154).

In 1910 DeForest organized a concert over radiotelephony by the Italian operatic tenor Enrico Caruso. The performance took place at the Metropolitan Opera House and was sent approximately thirteen miles away to Time Square, but anyone tuned to the same frequency caught the show.

Sarnoff advocated for programming for an audience. "I have in mind a plan of development which would make radio a household utility in the same sense as the piano or the phonograph. The idea is to bring music into the house by wireless" (Douglas 15). Sarnoff pitched his vision to his superiors at RCA, but they were focused on commercial radiotelegraphy and uninterested in point-to-mass communication. "[RCA] laughed at the idea that individual citizens would want to have radio receiving sets in their homes" (Douglas 78).

Nevertheless, Sarnoff persisted and proved his point on July 2, 1921, when he aired the boxing match between the American champion Jack Dempsey and French hero Georges Carpentier. This idea made history yet again for the radio. There were $60,000,000 worth of radio sales in 1922, and it more than doubled in 1923 to $136,000,000. Within three years following the boxing match, RCA alone sold approximately $80,000,000 worth of equipment. Towards the end of the decade in 1928, there were $650,550,000 worth of sets sold, and over 7.5 million homes had a radio set (Douglas 69, 75, 77).

Some stations continued to broadcast sports games. Some were run by doctors, universities, or preachers who gave lectures and sermons. Part of the programming usually involved the news and a weather report. One of the more notable radio personalities who debuted in 1923 was Dr. John R. Brinkley. He owned KFKB and used the airtime to promote his advanced transplant technique to reverse erectile dysfunction using goat glands. Despite the variety of programs available, music has always been the heart of radio.

The popularity of radio had almost an instant effect on the music industry. It created jobs for studio workers and musicians. Featuring live talent on air also transformed the studios themselves. Primitive production rooms could not even be called a studio. For example, a microphone and transmitter may be in a garage or in a tent on top of a roof. Thus, to attract live acts, station owners began investing more in the facility by building specialized sets with better acoustics for being on air. Studios also provided a piano for the performers, and most placed a lampshade over the microphone to pacify mike fright. Some stars even received a personal limousine to chauffeur them to the studio.

The music industry in turn motivated improvements in the quality of broadcasting. The famous announcer Thomas Cowan, who worked for WJZ in Newark, New Jersey, once received records from Thomas Edison to play on air, though Edison did not support the technology once he heard the sound quality. Soon Edwin Armstrong invented FM, as opposed to AM, which widened the bandwidth, refined the sound, and quieted the static. The caliber of microphones also improved. The standard in the early 1930s was RCA's 44A ribbon or "velocity," and a few years later RCA introduced the 77A cardioid pattern dual ribbon microphone bringing "subtlety and nuance" to broadcasters (*Big Bands and the Swing Era* par 11).

Before radio was ready to launch revolutions in music, someone had to reign in the chaos and traffic in the sky. As stations sprang up, issues multiplied. Programs desperately needed mandating. The surge in sales drove up the demand for talent. The main source of funding went undecided for several years. Finally, stations were challenged with differentiating their show from the multitude of others. Within two years of KDKA's premier there were over one hundred stations in the United States (Douglas 32).

Without regulating who could talk at what time using which frequency, managing air traffic was a disaster in the hands of private stations and individuals. Some stations broadcasted long past their allotted time. People didn't know when to tune in. Strangers eavesdropped on private conversations. Despite the effort to operate outside of government supervision, the need for a governing body, vastly led by the American Radio Relay League, became clear. Current Secretary of Commerce and future president Herbert Hoover tackled the problem.

Hoover called for the first Conference on Radio Telephony in 1922 in order to resolve the issue of the extent of government control. After World War I the Department of the Navy wanted control over the airwaves but management fell under the Department of Commerce. Initially, licensed broadcasters could only use the frequency 833kHz, and Hoover entrusted the public to work together to schedule themselves. He believed "that one should rely not on government but on civic minded individuals" and advocated for the power of civic duty, responsibility, and initiative (Leuchtenburg 31).

To Hoover's disappointment, stations were not able to privately organize themselves. Thus, he proposed new regulations at the radio conference. For example, he assigned certain bandwidths to different groups: one for army, one for navy, one for public stations, one for amateurs. Furthermore, each station received its own wavelength, until the number of stations outgrew the dial. This was the result of one of four radio conferences called by Hoover, and these modifications, though underdeveloped, promoted better shows and talent. Hoover also promoted live performances and live music and discouraged playing phonograph records over the air since families can listen to the phonograph in their own home any day.

Initially, classical music was the main entertainment on the radio and had a vast impact on society. Individuals who may not have had the chance to go to a concert were able to hear professional symphonies and entire operas. Furthermore, the public got a chance to hear soloists such as Jascha Heifetz and Sergei Rachmaninoff over the air when normally the orchestra in their city would not be able to afford such talent. A desire for music education later formed. Providing music education in school was rare in the twenties, but every school offered a music class by the late thirties.

An appreciation for classical music grew. There were 60 orchestras across the nation in 1928, and by 1930 there were nearly 300. Westinghouse built a second radio station in Chicago in 1921, KYW, and it was intended to exclusively broadcast opera. There were only 1,000 receivers in Chicago when it opened, but by the end of the opera season in 1922 there were approximately 20,000. After the season ended, managers had an open schedule to program. WLS in Chicago owned by Sears and Roebuck and Company filled the void with country music making Chicago the temporary country musical capital of the world.

Classical music had a strong relationship with the radio and was preferred over records since listeners could hear a symphony without the interruption of turning over or changing a disc. Other genres still heavily relied on record sales. Jazz was a prime example. The presence of jazz on the radio was minimal compared to classical and disproportionate to the number of jazz records that were selling. This reflected the conservative culture rather than the musical preferences at the time. People believed jazz to be forceful and taboo. No radio station wanted to be associated with it.

Still, "it was really dance band orchestras that the young wanted to hear…the young wanted played on the radio the same sorts of tunes that they were accustomed to hearing on phonograph records" (Douglas 169). Variety shows became popular as radio announcers and producers became more willing to cast a wider net of talent, so they took performers from vaudeville acts. "To give people the kind of music they wanted to hear you had to do it in a way that could be justified as simple light fare, and this was best done through a modification and toning down of traditional vaudeville routines" (Douglas 171-172).

The Ziegfeld Follies, a famous vaudeville-like traveling group, got their own show, *The Ziegfeld Follies of the Air,* which premiered in 1932. The orchestra was led by Al Goodman, and soloists included Fanny Brice and Jack Pearl. George White's Scandals, another variety show, launched the career of many radio stars such as Barbara Pepper and Alice Faye.

One unforgettable variety act was Rude Vallée's "The Fleischmann Hour." Born Hubert Prior Vallée, he taught himself saxophone influenced by Rudy Wiedoeft. He spent time in the vaudeville circuit and with Victor Lopez's orchestra. Vallée was discovered in the Heigh Ho Club on the east side of New York as a band member and singer.

The band caught WABC's ear who hired Vallée to be the announcer as well as lead musician for their new program live from the Heigh Ho Club. Perhaps just as famous as his music was his ability to enrapture women and his greeting, "Heigh-ho everybody!" (Rudel 222). Soon two more stations, WOR and WMCA, contracted out nights to record Vallée and his band. Vallée's career took off lightning fast and a year later, he got "The Fleischmann Hour," which held the top rating for its time slot for the next ten years.

Dance bands or orchestras promoted the acceptance of jazz. Vincent Lopez, invited by Tommy Cowan of WJZ, led the first dance band to play over the air. He was an established society band leader working in hotels, but by playing on the radio he encouraged the acceptance of the forbidden genre. Paul Whiteman, who was also a dance band leader in hotels, commissioned George Gershwin to compose a jazz piece for his orchestra. The result was the notorious work "Rhapsody in Blue," thus demonstrating that jazz is a respectable art form. During the latter half of the twenties, stations finally were able to broadcast the music of Lopez, Whiteman, Isham Jones, and Ted Lewis with soaring reviews.

Vaudeville had a bittersweet relationship with the radio. "In 1929 the vaudeville audience started to disappear, drawn away by the mechanized entertainment powerhouses of talking pictures and coast-to-coast radio programming. Ironically neither talking pictures nor radio, both of which came to maturity during the 1920s, would ever have become so popular without the foundation built by vaudeville" (Rudel 200-201). Some individuals go as far as claiming that radio killed vaudeville.

Swing developed a similar story because of the radio. It evolved from the sinful jazz of the 1920s, which had roots in Dixieland and Delta blues. The early blues were characterized by smaller ensembles, appropriately sized to perform in limited spaces such as on a boat. As the jazz of Duke Ellington, Ben Pollack, and Fletcher Henderson grew in popularity and acceptance, so too did ensembles grow into "big bands." Groups found a home in clubs and hotel dance ballrooms, which often had a radio wire to broadcast live music. Benny Goodman, Coleman Hawkins, and Glenn Miller rose to prominence in the thirties sweeping in the style of swing. Goodman himself kicked off the Swing Era in 1935 at the Palomar Ballroom in Los Angeles, California.

Sadly, this era ended after The Recording Ban of 1942-1944 and as a repercussion of World War II. Despite Hoover's criticism of airing recorded music, stations depended on records. Once stations needed to schedule longer programs, they turned to playing music from a phonograph in order to help fill time. In the early forties, "60% of all the country's radio stations depended on records to exist—that without them they would go under" (Levin 2).

The use of phonographs provoked an unintended consequence from disgruntled performers. Musicians and composers fought against stations airing their art without being able to collect the royalties they deserved. In 1942 the instrumentalists formed a union in the American Federation of Musicians to combat this injustice. They boycotted recording studios so the studios could no longer play their records on air. During this period, musicians relied on live gigs for income.

Their efforts to support themselves with live jobs were derailed by World War II. Thousands of male musicians enlisted to serve, the government placed a "cabaret tax" on live entertainment, and a curfew was put into effect at clubs and ballrooms. Thus, most big bands met too many obstacles to find work and ensembles shrank in size to a small combo of "scab" musicians. This usually consisted of a piano, bass, drums, and sometimes a saxophone. Dizzy Gillespie and Charlie Parker were products of this era and ushered in the age of bebop. The war also highlighted all-female groups such as the Hour of Charm Orchestra and the International Sweethearts of Rhythm.

Because war radio stations depended even more heavily on recorded music yet were at a stalemate because of The Recording Ban, producers, fraught for content, turned to what was available. Because vocalists were exempt from the AFM, stations hired more vocalists, gifted and inept alike, and featured vocal recordings. The big band era therefore dwindled, and bebop and the group vocal sound of the fifties was born.

The radio had survived two world wars and a nationwide strike by musicians, but now it faced another point of contention that could break the industry: how to fund a medium that was supposed to be free to the public. The Secretary of Commerce, Herbert Hoover, was put in charge to find funding.

As with corralling airway traffic, Hoover skirted a fine line between allowing radio to be an enterprise free of government interference and creating a body to delegate finances. One idea was to erect municipal studios so cities controlled the money, while another was to place a tax on radio sets, which would be turned over to a central station to distribute.

Hoover feared the airwaves would be polluted by commercials, so direct advertising was not allowed. "It is inconceivable that we should allow so great a possibility for service to be drowned in advertising chatter" (Rudel 56). Many of the groups acquired a sponsor in place of advertising, e.g., the Lucky Strike Orchestra, the Silvertown Cord Orchestra, and the Kodak Chorus. Some businesses commissioned a jingle about their product to circumvent direct advertising but still make their name memorable. The Wheaties Quartet sang the first ever jingle in 1926 to promote the Wheaties breakfast cereal.

Ads and product placement inevitably crept into programs. Finally, NBC, the oldest major broadcasting company in the United States formed by none other than RCA President David Sarnoff, pushed the line between direct and indirect advertising beyond distinction. By the 1930s funding by advertising was the rule, not the exception.

Radio stations constantly worked to maintain talent and funding, and the last piece of the puzzle was to attract listeners. The country was a captivated audience, so the number of fans was not the issue; the radio played for over 90 million listeners in its golden age in the 1930s. Rather, there were too many stations to choose from, and listeners often didn't know which were airing at any given time.

In the late forties, Gordon McLendon, who owned KLIF, made a decision that solved this issue and set the trend for every station around the world. He decided to utilize the studio band in a greater capacity beyond just singing jingles for advertisers and sponsors.

> *That morphed into singing about the show itself...it was a jingle for the radio station. They would use them as fillers in case a show ran short...They're also used to make one station sound different than another...[and] the jingles are supposed to be a catchy way to get that call letter or the name of the station in your mind with a little*

catchy melody so you know what it is...And the reason that's important is because radio stations for the most part make their money by selling advertising, and the more listeners they have the more they can charge for those commercials.

Jonathan Wolfert, President of JAM Creative Productions, Inc.

Personal interview April 27, 2021

Most every station eventually commissioned or created their own ID. Singing tunes about the station increased name recognition, distinguished one station from another, allowed for stations to receive better ratings, and therefore boosted the profit. This helped to extend the lifespan of radio in the face of television, but its popularity dwindled towards the end of the twentieth century.

The radio made history. It was a "box that connected [people] to the world." The radio reported history "[making] America a land of listened. It entertained and educated...angered and delighted Americans of every kind and age and class." And finally, it became history. Television quickly dominated the entertainment field. Norman Corwin, a writer and director of radio drama, said, "When people speak of the golden age of radio, they're speaking of the shortest golden age in history. It's golden years perhaps covered a decade, little more than that, maybe 15 years, and it was cut short by the release of television" (Burns *Empire of the Air*).

Radio may have lost to advances in technology, but it is not extinct. KDKA celebrated its 100th anniversary on November 2, 2020. As of March 2021, there were over 15,000 licensed commercial broadcast stations in the United States according to the Federal Communications Commission. Radio is a symbol of free speech and a reflection of America's tastes, values, and potential. Its history intertwines with music and there will forever be synergy between the two domains. Roger Taylor, drummer of Queen, said it best. "You had your time. You had the power. You've yet to have your finest hour.... Radio, what's new? Someone still loves you."

————

To conclude my story, I want to thank Jonathan Wolfert, President of JAM Creative Productions, Inc. in Dallas, TX. Jon took the time to explain what takes place behind the scenes at the recording studio. I also got to hear the story of how he went from a kid with a dream to a young man with wild hair who just opened his own recording studio. (Yes, Jon, I saw your throwback photo on Facebook from the 70s). I was not able to incorporate all of the information from the interview but having a better understanding of radio jingles helped guide this essay.

Works Cited

Big Bands and the Swing Era. Leonard Wyeth & Acoustic Music.Org, 2008, https://acousticmusic.org/research/history/musical-styles-and-venues-in-america/big-bands-and-the-swing-era/. Accessed 1 June 2021.

Federal Communications Commission; *Broadcast Station Totals as of March 31, 2021*; Federal Communications Commission, 5 April 2021.

Douglas, George H. *The Early Days of Radio Broadcasting.* McFarland Classics, 1987.

The Early Days of Radio. Museum of American Heritage, 18 Feb. 2003, http://www.moah.org/radio/earlydays.html#:~:text=But%20it%20was%20the%20Italian,the%20Atlantic%20Ocean%20in%201902. Accessed 1 June 2021.

Empire of the Air: The Men Who Made Radio. Directed by Kenneth Burns, narrated by Jason Robards, Florentine Films, 1991.

Leuchtenburg, William. *Herbert Hoover*. Times Books, 2009.

Levin, Mike. "All Recording Stops Today." *DownBeat*. 1 August 1942, pg. 1-2.

Roger Taylor. "Radio Ga Ga." *The Works,* Record Plant, 1984.

Rudel, Anthony. *Hello, Everybody!: The Dawn of American Radio.* Hardcourt Books, 2008.

Vincent Lopez — Grill Room 1954. Craig's BigBand and Big-Names, 2003, https://www.bigbandsandbignames.com/lopez.html. Accessed 15 June 2021.

Wolfert, Jonathan. Personal interview. 27 April 2021.

THE ORIGINS OF MY MUSICAL JOURNEY

Edwin Lacy

It is 1943, and the world-shaking events of World War II seem far removed from here, an isolated farm in rural Southwestern Kentucky. Today is a humid Sunday in mid-July, with a temperature in the high 90s, and the sun beats down unmercifully on the farm crops.

On the farm is a two-story white frame farmhouse, barely altered since it was built in the nineteenth century. Large trees shade the house, providing some welcome relief from the stifling heat. There is no electricity in the house, as the rural electrification project has not yet reached this remote area. Nor is there running water, only a cistern behind the house that collects rainwater. The toilet facility is a shabby structure in the backyard. The only heat in the winter is a coal-burning fireplace in the room that is most often occupied, and a similarly fueled stove in the kitchen. The floors are well-worn rough planks, and the furnishings are simple and mostly hand-made. The only evidence of the twentieth century is a crank telephone hanging on the wall in the entrance hall.

Today there is a family gathering. The members of the large extended family have not strayed far from the places of their birth, and nearly all the living relatives are here—grandparents to grandchildren, cousins, aunts and uncles, and their spouses and children—nearly thirty people. It is Sunday, and after the daily required chore of taking care of their farm animals, everybody has gone to church before coming to the farm for the reunion. Men have removed their coast but, despite the heat, leave on their white shirts and ties. Some arrive in their aging cars or farm trucks, while others, who live closer, arrive on their farm wagons drawn by mules, as it is difficult to buy car tires and gasoline due to the wartime economy.

The first thing that occupies everybody's attention is the family dinner, for which everyone has contributed. There is more food than the entire group could eat in several days: fried chicken, ham, and other meats are plentiful; fried fish as someone had good luck fishing in their farm ponds and nearby streams; potatoes, fresh tomatoes, several kinds of beans and peas, and other vegetables, all grown on the family's farms. For dessert there is coconut cake, chocolate cake, various kinds of fruit pies, and more. The food is displayed on a makeshift table, planks placed across sawhorses in the shade of a tree, covered by cloths to keep flies and other insects from the food until it is time to eat.

Chairs for the senior adults are in the shade of the trees while younger people sit on the spacious front porch or on the ground. After eating, the adults retire to the large parlor of the house, the men first while the women put away the food and wash the dishes. The plentiful leftovers are divided among the families, each putting their bounty for the meals of the next few days in the containers in which they have brought their own contributions to the meal.

After the women join the group in the parlor, casual conversation ensues about friends and family members, the prices that farm crops are likely to bring this year, who is suffering from various maladies, and, of course, the hot weather; several vigorously fan themselves with paper fans bearing nature images or messages from local funeral homes or other businesses. As almost all are farmers, they are concerned about how severe this year's near-annual drought will be.

Although these people, particularly the older ones, have little education, they read newspapers. The few who have radios listen to the news. They are aware of world events, and they discuss the progress of the War. The outcome of the events taking place around the world is by no means assured, and parents begin to contemplate the possibility that their teenaged children may have to join the military.

Soon, musical instruments are brought out. While nobody has had any formal musical training, many in the group play instruments—guitars, fiddles, even a mandolin or a banjo—played in effective if unorthodox ways, perhaps taught by older relatives who themselves may have been self-taught. There is a piano in the parlor, as there is in nearly every home, and several people can play it. After a lengthy discussion about what song to play and sing, somebody begins a familiar church hymn, sung in the church services earlier that day, followed by another and another; "Dwelling in Beulah Land," "Bringing in the Sheaves," "What a Friend We Have in Jesus," "Standing on the Promises," all sung in the rural churches for generations. With "The Old Rugged Cross," a favorite, the singing becomes more fervent, the harmonies more lush. Eventually, someone remembers their dear departed mother, and requests "That Silver-Haired Mother of Mine." Many a cheek shows evidence of tears during the singing of this one, and some voices begin to crack with emotion.

When they run out of hymns to request, the musicians segue into traditional folk songs brought to Kentucky by their ancestors from the mountains of Virginia and the Carolinas: "Red River Valley," "Cotton-Eyed Joe," "The Ballad of John Henry," and "Cripple Creek." These songs are more rhythmic and upbeat, and the mood of the group grows lighter.

Most of the children show little interest in the musical offering, and the sound of their playing in the yard drifts through the open windows. Periodically they are asked to move their games farther from the house.

This notable day took place a few weeks before my sixth birthday. But I did not join the children in the yard because for as long as I can remember I have been fascinated and transfixed by music, almost magnetically attracted to any musical sound. As I listen, I forget anything else that may have been on my mind. On this day, I sat quietly while intently listening to the proceedings. As primitive as the day's music may have been, the harmonies were miraculous to me. I recognized what I learned much later in life as simple harmonic progressions, simple meters, and verse-and-chorus formal structure. Before long, I learned to read music by following the music in the church hymnal and by observing the musical symbols as I became progressively better at deciphering them.

Eventually, my family left the farm and moved to the nearby town. Life was hardly less of a struggle there, but one of our few possessions was a table model radio, given to us by a family member who had bought a new one. There was only one mode of broadcast, AM, but classical music could sometimes be heard on the radio. At the age of six or seven, I would scan the dial until I found a symphony orchestra playing. I asked my mother what this kind of music was called. She wasn't sure, but I said, "That's the kind of music I am going to play when I grow up." To this day, I don't know how I determined that resolve would guide my life.

Sometimes I did chores for my grandparents or neighbors for a few cents. When I saved enough, I went to the "5 and 10 cent" store and bought a simple musical instrument similar to a fife. There was a fingering chart and a few simple songs in the fife's instruction booklet. I practiced interminably, driving my parents to distraction, until I learned all the songs. Then I performed little recitals for my family. My mother and father were impressed that I could do that, even without the benefit of instruction, and they began to realize that there might be a future in music for me, as foreign a path as that seemed to my family.

I availed myself of any opportunity to hear music of almost any kind. There was a semi-professional baseball team in our town of Hopkinsville, Kentucky. I normally couldn't afford the ten cents that a child's ticket would cost, but I stood outside the baseball park to hear the music played on loudspeakers between innings, often Sousa marches.

Finally, it became time for fifth grade students in my elementary school to have the opportunity to join the band program. I wanted to join them and begged my parents at length to obtain an instrument for me. I had decided that I would play the clarinet, for what seemed to me a very good reason: a girl that I wanted to be my girlfriend played the clarinet. I realize now that part of my parents' reluctance was that the entire experience of music was so far from the reality of their lives that they couldn't conceive of why it would be so important to me. In any case, there was no possibility of them being able to buy a clarinet for me. That would cost about $125 and would be the most expensive thing that our family had ever purchased. Eventually, after another year of urging on my part my parents realized that I was indeed serious about my desire to study music. So, they relented and made the great sacrifice to buy the clarinet for me. I'm sure it took years for them to pay for it.

Even though I joined the band program a year later than my peers, due to my enthusiasm for the music and my faithful practice, I soon caught up and overtook the other students of my age. After a year of playing the clarinet, my band director needed an oboe player and decided that I would be the person to learn that instrument. Still another year later, I added saxophone to my arsenal of instruments so that I could play it in marching band and jazz band. It wasn't until I entered college to study music that I began playing the bassoon, the instrument that would occupy so much of my time and hard work over the years, and which provided me with so much pleasure.

These experiences of more than three-quarters of a century ago started me on a path that I have never deviated from. Nor have I ever lost the enthusiasm for music that I discovered so long ago. Music has been central to my life and has provided me with much joy and satisfaction. I can't conceive of doing anything else.

CHOIR BOY AT LARGE

John O'Leary

I can't remember a time before singing.

I imagine my first, full-throated tone ensued from a slap on my bottom, prompting my father to say "gee." To which an attending nurse replied, "I think it was an F."

My family wasn't especially musical. I learned just recently, leafing through an antique yearbook, that my mother played the clarinet. I never heard her mention it. Nor did I ever hear her sing. I do recall her working in the kitchen with the radio on, Glenn Miller's *Moonlight Serenade* among the melodies beaming from a tower on Mount Auburn Road. My dad's musicality was more apparent. He always toted a tune around, whistling or humming as he went about whatever task was at hand. Standing beside him at Sunday Mass I was privy to a bright, clear baritone, pitch-true and warm. He credited his mother's musical giftedness for his own. If a genetic thread knits my family's songsters, it surely runs through Mary Francis O'Leary (née Beer).

The Christmas season wrapped me in a garland of melodies. Traditional carols, such as *Silent Night*, *Hark! The Herald Angels Sing*, and *O Come All Ye Faithful* swept me to the manger. Music made the Nativity story more real, more wonderful. I delighted, too, in elegant, pop perennials; *The Christmas Song*

(*Chestnuts*), *Do You Hear What I Hear?* and *White Christmas* still jockey for the top of my list. Although I sang along with some of the novelties, *Rudolph* and *Frosty the Snowman*, in general they struck me as one-trick ponies—no need for a second listen. *All I Want for Christmas Is My Two Front Teeth* was the most wearisome of them all the year I lost my own front teeth. Every adult I encountered would assert, with a tiresome wink, they knew just what *I* wanted for Christmas.

I suppose my aversion to kitsch, in combination with a simmering wish to sing before an audience, set me up for my first public performance. The venue was my first-grade classroom at Christ the King grade school on an afternoon in December. Sister Bernadine announced we were in for a special treat and called forward a classmate who took his place in front. With the confidence of Caruso, he delivered a raspy, Alfalfa-esque rendition of *Nuttin' for Christmas*. It was my first hearing of the song, and I didn't care much for it, especially the image of ants in a sugar bowl. I perceived a shabby gauntlet, and I reflexively picked it up.

"I know a Christmas carol," I blurted as my hand shot up.

"Well, class, it seems John has a song, too," Sister said. "Please come up and sing it for us."

I hurried to the front and, facing my peers, poured out the most deeply felt interpretation of *O Little Town of Bethlehem* to ever waft *a capella* into mortal ears. Every note was pitch-perfect, every syllable formed with utmost clarity. My phrasing, timing, poise . . . all flawless. Or so I tell myself. In reality, I have no memory of the actual performance. It was obliterated on the spot, gone in an instant like the sung notes themselves, vanished forever into the ether. All because, as I returned to my desk, a girl pointed at the front of my trousers.

"Your zipper is open."

I glanced down in horror at a gaping fly. In that moment, no suit on any department-store Santa was any redder than my face. I had just learned what every singer who dares the nakedness of soloing must: *You're never perfect.* You miss an entrance. Your voice cracks. Your costume malfunctions. There are more ways to flub a performance than there are cheeks in the bleachers at a Kiss concert. Either your hide thickens, or you wilt. Fear embarrassment, and you're already doomed. As Jay Leno said when asked what to do if a joke falls flat: *Get used to it.*

I recall an Evansville Philharmonic Orchestra Christmas Pops Concert some years ago where the featured vocalist, a baritone with an impressive résumé in film and commercial work, mangled the lyrics on *My Favorite Things*. He didn't just miss a syllable or two; he scrambled and served the words like geese paper packages tied up in wings. But he was a real pro, and at the song's conclusion he gave an impromptu aside: "One of my favorite things is remembering the words to that song." The audience laughed. On with the show.

A convent with a bevy of Benedictine nuns graced the campus of Christ the King. The sisters accounted for about 90 percent of the school's teaching staff, including two full-time instructors in music. I suppose my caroling put me on their radar because I was soon drafted into the alto section of the boys choir. Singing was routine for every student. Latin plainsong, intrinsic to pre-Vatican II rituals, was a given in the school's daily celebration of the Mass. The Kyriale, a compact book of Gregorian notation for the Ordinary, was more commonplace in the pews than were handkerchiefs.

The liturgical year reached a musical zenith at midnight on Christmas with a high Mass sung from the gallery by an SATB choir of men and boys. I recently paid a visit to that loft, my first after a hiatus of more than 50 years. It no longer opens to the nave, having ceded its connection decades ago in a remodeling that brought musicians onto the floor of the sanctuary; now it serves as storage for a miscellany of seasonal decorations and accoutrements of worship.

Stepping into the space where the risers once stood, I visualized a group of 40 bow-tied boys with burr haircuts and butch-waxed flattops, standing in three rows. Behind them, in two rows, 16 well-groomed men in coats and ties filled out the bass and tenor sections. Mrs. Wathen, in a blue floral dress, her silver hair impeccably coiffed, sat at the organ, fingers kneading the keys. Her gaze was ever shifting, just slightly, from her music to the director and back again. On the director's dais, Mr. Handley, with the sleeves of his white shirt rolled up to his elbows and perspiration dripping from every pore, glided his milky arms through the air, coaxing and pulling from the skein of voices to weave a sonic tapestry. Our beloved teachers, Sisters Bernadette and Julius, faces radiant inside their black-and-white habits, stood to the side, following along in their scores.

They cast their eyes with diligent regularity at the boys sections, attentive to every sound and movement of their young charges and ready to intervene with a tissue or cough drop or to okay an urgent trip to the lavatory. And, from deep in the risers, somewhere in tenor land, came the unmistakable timbre of Mr. Chamberlain's voice, captivating the entire assembly with a rapturous solo on *O Holy Night*.

Oh, halcyon days.

That early schooling has provided a priceless passport. Like a golden ticket from Willy Wonka, I have tendered it for admittance to more than one factory where the sweets are savored only by the ears. In 1999, it took me to a baritone chair with Germania Männerchor as we prepared for the society's centennial celebration. I was a triple-dipper then; I had joined the Philharmonic Chorus the year before, and I was a regular in my parish choir. It added up to a minimum of three rehearsals a week with three vastly different groups.

The focus of my parish choir was, naturally, praise and worship. Anyone could join, regardless of ability; God's children all, everyone makes a joyful noise. Most of the music was fairly simple, geared primarily toward participation by the congregation. By contrast, the Philharmonic Chorus was dedicated to artistic interpretation. Joining required an audition. Some were classically trained vocalists, and all were capable sight readers. Rehearsals began with about 15 minutes of warmup— body stretching, neck and shoulder massage, and exercises for breathing, vocalization, and articulation. Musical selections ranged from moderately challenging to difficult. A disciplined work ethic prevailed; members shared high expectations and pushed for perfection.

My German friends marched to the beat of a different glockenspiel. The audition consisted of a few rehearsals with the group before it offered an invitation to join. The practice room adjoined a rathskeller, and beer washed easily across bass and tenor tonsils alike. A long-standing wisecrack posited that we couldn't decide if we were a singing society that liked to drink—or a drinking society that liked to sing. Regardless, when we put our minds to it, we could soar in streaming, golden harmonies to rival the seraphim. On occasion, a concert goer would ask me how an Irishman had gotten mixed up with the group. I would quip that my name was actually "O'Leary-hausen." Or, maybe it was the "Beer" in my pedigree. In any case, I shared my colleagues' pride in Deutsche Lied and a culture that produced so many titans of Western music.

During the 1990s, the advance of desktop computing and software for music notation encouraged me to commit musical ideas to print. My associates were receptive, and it thrilled me to hear them perform my work, even my primitive efforts. With each new piece, I became more confident that my creations had merit. If not destined for immortality in the canon of choral masterpieces, they might at least provide a degree of fresh enjoyment for my fellow singers and our audiences. (A caveat: If you happen upon my arrangement of *I Saw Three Ships*, please do me a favor and shred it. Immediately.)

One evening, Germania's president asked me to think about writing a song that would speak to the immigrant experience of German families. He wondered if many who settled in the Evansville area had come from the valleys of Germany's great rivers. Maybe our little pocket of the Ohio reminded them of their native land. I thought this an interesting angle and agreed to see if I could develop it. The song took shape as *Beautiful River*, and the Männerchor and Damenchor performed it in a subsequent concert cycle.

Beautiful River

They crossed the cold and dark Atlantic;

They came ashore in search of their dreams.

Hearts filled with hope and patient yearning,

They wended west, tracing native streams.

They carried mem'ries of the Rhineland

And of the Danube, tranquil and blue.

So, when they spied the wide Ohio,

They saw the fatherland anew.

Beautiful River, you are my story.

Your restless spirit feels like my own.

I see my life in your meandering;

Your nurt'ring valley, my beloved home.

I am a child of freedom, wandering,

Her daring daughter, her roving son,

Part of a flood of restless dreamers;

Beautiful River, we are one.

Beautiful River, sweet, drifting destiny,

My lot is cast forever on your shore.

Beautiful River, course of humanity,

My heart is yours forevermore.

I am a child of freedom, wandering,

Her daring daughter, her roving son,

A restless tide of wide-eyed dreamers;

Beautiful River, we are one.

Wir sind eins, O schöne Fluß, **Beautiful River!**

I have since revisited the composition and arranged it for solo voice with piano accompaniment. In closing this essay, I offer it as a gift, along with the wish that you and I will some-day find ourselves in the same chorus. In the meantime, let's keep singing.

To download sheet music for *Beautiful River*, use the camera on your mobile device to capture this code.

Or go to: www.birdbrainpublishing.com/beautiful-river.

TRIP THE SELF-POETRUSIC

James D. Casey IV

listening to Miles
run the voodoo down
clacking the keys
between his notes
sliding through
the folds of my mind

i get lost
in the music
get lost
in thought
lost in words

lost

to myself

looking for myself
inside myself

here i find
the pirates
and the ghosts
and the villains

rooted for
in youth

now dining
with the demons
picked up
along my chosen
path

all nodding
in solidarity
behind twisted smiles

and i know
they will keep
my secrets
safe

and i know
the notes
will carry me
home

Contributors

Melanie Baker, an Evansville native, currently works as the Director of Worship at Good Shepherd Catholic Parish. A 2019 graduate of the University of Evansville, Melanie was involved in the University Choir, Jazz Ensemble I, and the Gumberts Competition, and she was the winner of the 2017 Vukovich Concerto Competition. Melanie now directs adult and children's choirs at Good Shepherd, teaches piano lessons privately, and performs as a freelance musician.

Tony Brewer is a poet, live sound effects artist, and event producer. He is executive director of the Spoken Word Stage at the 4th Street Arts Festival, co-producer of the Writers Guild Spoken Word Series, and president of the National Audio Theatre Festivals. His writing has appeared in *Ryder Magazine, Laureate, Seppuku Quarterly, Voices from the Fire, Rye Whiskey Review, Fevers of the Mind, Northwest Indiana Literary Journal, Pulp Poets Press, The Beatnik Cowboy, Punk Noir Magazine*, and elsewhere and he has been nominated twice for a Pushcart Prize. He frequently collaborates with experimental audio collective Urban Deer Recording Cvlt and he has produced and recorded for KKFI, KOPN, and WFHB community radio and WFIU public radio as well as NPR Playhouse and the HEAR Now Audio Fiction & Arts Festival. His books include: *The Great American Scapegoat, Little Glove in a Big Hand, Hot Type Cold Read, Homunculus,* and *The History of Projectiles.* He also appears in the anthologies *A Linen Weave of Bloomington Poets, And Know This Place: Poetry of*

Indiana, *Writers Resist: Hoosier Writers Unite*, *Death by Punk*, and on the Urban Deer album *Paris Suite*.

Dr. Emily Britton served as Principal Horn of the Evansville Philharmonic from 2015 to 2021, during which time she was also on the faculty of the University of Evansville. Currently teaching horn at the University of Louisville, she maintains a busy freelancing schedule, including the positions of principal horn of the Owensboro Symphony Orchestra, Guest Principal Horn of the Indianapolis Chamber Orchestra, third horn of the Evansville Philharmonic. She is a frequent substitute in the Louisville Orchestra, Orchestra Kentucky of Bowling Green, and the Nashville Scoring Orchestra. Previously, Dr. Britton was a member of the USAF Heritage of America Band. She earned a Doctor of Music from Florida State University.

Joshua Britton is the author of *Tadpoles*, a recently published collection of twelve short stories, and has published fiction and non-fiction in numerous journals, including *Tethered by Letters*, *The Bombay Review*, *Cobalt Review*, *The Journal of the International Trombone Association*, and *The Tarantino Chronicles* (see full list at www.joshua-britton.com). As a tenor and bass trombonist, Joshua has performed with many ensembles, including the Evansville Philharmonic Orchestra, the Owensboro Symphony Orchestra, the Orchestra Kentucky Bowling Green, the Louisville Orchestra, Shepard Brass, River Brass, Tidewater Winds, Virginia Beach Symphony Orchestra, Tallahassee Symphony Orchestra, and Northwest Florida Symphony Orchestra. In 2019, at the North American Brass Band Association in Fort Wayne, Indiana, Joshua won first place in the Technical Solo

Division. Joshua earned a Bachelor of Science in Music Education from Roberts Wesleyan College and a Master's in Trombone performance from Florida State University. A father of two, Joshua is a fan of the Pittsburgh Pirates, spaghetti westerns, novelist Philip Roth, and red-headed horn players.

James D. Casey IV is an artist, award-winning poet, author of seven poetry collections, and the founder/editor-in-chief of <u>Cajun Mutt Press</u>. His work can be found in print and online at several small press venues and literary magazines internationally.

Thomas Drury is a native of Carlinville, Illinois and has lived in Evansville, Indiana since 2004. He studied piano and organ at the University of Iowa and collaborative piano at the University of Michigan. He holds various posts in the Evansville music community, teaching music at the University of Southern Indiana, serving as organist at Trinity United Methodist Church, accompanying the Evansville Philharmonic Chorus, and playing in various local jazz groups, including his own Tom Drury Quartet. He is married to soprano and choral director Andrea Drury and is the proud father of three sons.

John Guzlowski is a poet and novelist whose works have been reviewed in the premier newspapers in the United States. His most recent works are *True Confessions*, a book of autobiographical poems, and *Little Altar Boy*, a mystery novel dealing with pedophilia. He is also a columnist for the Dziennik Zwiazkowy, the oldest Polish newspaper in America.

Tim Heerdink is the author of *Somniloquy & Trauma in the Knottseau Well*, *The Human Remains*, *Red Flag and Other Poems*, *Razed Monuments*, *Checking Tickets on Oumaumua*, *Sailing the Edge of Time*, *I Hear a Siren's Call*, *Ghost Map*, *A Cacophony of Birds in the House of Dread*, and short stories, *The Tithing of Man* and *HEA-VEN2*. His poems appear in various journals and anthologies. He is the President of Midwest Writers Guild of Evansville, Indiana

Bill Hemminger taught English, French, and Russian at University of Evansville until his retirement a few years ago. Bill is a pianist, composer, gardener, poet, and active community volunteer in addition to his academic work. His essay, "Our Song In Africa," arises from his work as Fulbright Professor of Literature in several African nations. Bill has edited a book published by Indiana University Press called *Growing Good: A Beginner's Guide to Creating Caring Communities*. He has also been a regular contributor to the Evansville Courier-Press, where he reviews Evansville Philharmonic Orchestra concerts.

Jenny Kalahar is the editor and publisher of *Last Stanza Poetry Journal*. She is the founding leader of Last Stanza Poetry Association in Elwood, Indiana, now in its tenth year. Jenny and her husband, poet Patrick, are used and rare booksellers. She was the humor columnist for *Tails Magazine* for several years and the treasurer for Poetry Society of Indiana. She is the author of fourteen books; her latest novel series is set in central Indiana. Twice nominated for a Pushcart Prize, her poems have been published in *Tipton Poetry Journal*, *Indiana Voice Journal*,

Trillium, Polk Street Review, Flying Island, and in several anthologies and newspapers. Her works can be found on poemhunter.com and *INverse,* Indiana's poetry archive. She and Patrick previously owned bookshops in Michigan and Ohio. Through her publishing house, Stackfreed Press, she has published books in the US and UK. jennykalahar@att.net

Patrick Kalahar is a used and rare bookseller with his wife, Jenny, and a book conservationist. He is a veteran, a world traveler, an avid reader, and a book collector. His poems have been published in *Tipton Poetry Journal, Flying Island, Rail Lines, The Moon and Humans, Polk Street Review, Northwest Indiana Literary Journal,* and *A Disconsolate Planet.*

A five-time recipient of the Solti Foundation U.S. Career Assistance Award (2013, 2017, 2018, 2020, 2021), **Roger Kalia** is the Music Director of the Evansville Philharmonic Orchestra, Symphony NH (Symphony New Hampshire), and Orchestra Santa Monica. He is also the Co-Founder and Music Director of the celebrated Lake George Music Festival in upstate New York, which celebrates its ten-year anniversary in August 2021. As the sixth music director of the Evansville Philharmonic Orchestra, Kalia reimagined the 2020-21 season with great success. His inaugural concert as music director featured the world premiere of Paul Dooley's *River City,* which celebrated both the Philharmonic and the city of Evansville. Kalia's innovative programming has included works by living composers such as Jessie Montgomery, Jessica Meyer, T.J. Cole, and Reena Esmail as well as unique collaborations and projects with

Evansville Civic Theatre, Historic Bosse Field, the Evansville World War 2 Museum, Ballet Indiana, and tango dancers from the University of Evansville. Kalia was recently recognized in the League of American Orchestra's *Symphony Magazine* as one of five first-year music directors for his innovative work during the pandemic. A native of New York State, Kalia holds degrees from Indiana University, the University of Houston and SUNY Potsdam's Crane School of Music. He is married to musicologist / violinist Christine Wisch.

Fr. Jeremy King, OSB, is a Benedictine monk and priest of Saint Meinrad Archabbey in Spencer County. He currently serves as one of the cantors and organists for the community liturgies. He also served as choirmaster for fourteen years over two terms in the office. He taught liturgy and sacraments in the seminary college and school of theology and was Director of Liturgy and Music in both schools. He served in parishes near Saint Meinrad for over twelve years, as well as for two years at what is now Saint Benedict Cathedral in Evansville. Fr. Jeremy King offers a memory of the years that Saint Meinrad Archabbey participated in the EPO Chorus beginning in 1984.

Reverend James Koressel was born on the west side of Evansville, IN in 1943, the twelfth of his parents' twelve children. He attended Sacred Heart School in Evansville, graduated from St. Joseph School in Evansville, and, in 1957, enrolled at St. Meinrad High School where his education continued for the next twelve years. Reverend Koressel received a Bachelor's Degree in Classics from St. Meinrad College and a Master of

Divinity Degree from St. Meinrad School of Theology. He was ordained to the Roman Catholic Priesthood in 1969. Since retiring from parish ministry in 2019, he resides in Evansville's west side.

Dr. Edwin Lacy, a native of Hopkinsville, Kentucky, received his Bachelor's degree in Music Education from Murray State University. After teaching for six years in the public schools of Indiana and Illinois, he attended Indiana University, earning a Master's degree in Bassoon Performance in 1966 and Doctor of Music in Woodwinds in 1978. He performed in the Evansville Philharmonic Orchestra from 1959 until recently, becoming the longest serving member in the history of that organization. In 1967 he joined the faculty of the Music Department at the University of Evansville where he continues to teach, also becoming the longest serving faculty member in the history of UE. He has been a visiting professor at the University of Louisville, Indiana University, and Southern Illinois University in Carbondale. He resides in Evansville with his wife of more than 60 years, Beverly, a retired music teacher and church organist.

Dr. Dennis Malfatti is Professor of Music and Director of Choral Activities at the University of Evansville. Choirs under his direction have sung by invitation at the American Choral Directors Association Central Division Conference in Chicago, at state level music education conferences in both Virginia and Indiana, and at Washington National Cathedral in Washington D.C. Twice he was invited to conduct performances of major choral-orchestral works at Carnegie Hall in New York with the

New England Symphonic Ensemble and festival choirs. He was founder and conductor of the Evansville Bach Singers, an auditioned chamber choir and professional chamber orchestra specializing in the sacred cantatas of J.S. Bach. He served for four seasons as Conductor of the Evansville Philharmonic Chorus and for four years as the chorus master and assistant conductor of the *Operafestival di Roma* (Italy.) As a participant in both the 2005 and 2010 Oregon Bach Festival conducting master classes, he studied choral/orchestral works of J.S. Bach with renowned conductor Helmuth Rilling and conducted the Oregon Bach Festival Orchestra and Chorus in several performances as part of the Discovery Series. He has published articles in state, regional, and national publications of the American Choral Directors Association. Most notably, his full-length article "Handel's *Saul*: The Apotheosis of Baroque Music-Theatre" was the featured cover article in the April 2018 edition of the *Choral Journal*. He is past president of the Indiana Choral Directors Association. A native of California, Dennis lives in Evansville, IN with his wife Celia and their daughter Annamaria.

John William McMullen is a writer, theologian, and a student of literature and the arts. In addition to his love for Bach, his musical interests vary from Gregorian Chant and Classical to Bluegrass and Rock. He is the author of *The Miracle of Stalag 8A—Beauty Beyond the Horror: Olivier Messiaen and the Quartet for the End of Time* and other books. McMullen lives in Evansville, Indiana, with his wife, Mary Grace.

Mary Grace Bernardin McMullen is the author of a collection of poetry, short stories, and the novel *Odd Numbers.* In addition to writing, she serves as a hospital chaplain for Ascension St. Vincent Evansville/Warrick. She is an avid music lover, much of her writing being inspired by diverse types of music; everything from Tchaikovsky, Debussy, and Rachmaninov to The Who, Joni Mitchell, and Johnny Cash. She enjoys reading, watching movies, hanging out with family and friends, and taking long walks with her beloved cocker spaniel, Deuce. Currently she is working on a new novel. She resides in Evansville with her husband, John.

John Michael O'Leary is a choir boy in Evansville, Indiana. Still at large, he was recently spotted in the loft at St. Benedict Cathedral. You can reach him at writerjmo.com.

Patsy Rahn's poetry and prose have been published in various journals and anthologies. Her book of poetry titled *The Grainy Wet Soul,* is available through several bookstores online. You can visit her author website at www.patsyrahn.com to hear some of her readings and sound works. You can also visit her photography website at www.skillfullycurledgphotography.com. Patsy Rahn worked for many years as an actress in Toronto, New York, and Los Angeles. She has a degree in political science from UCLA and a Master's degree in East Asian Languages and Cultures from Indiana University. She is a founding member and chairperson emerita of the Writers Guild at Bloomington.

Maestro Alfred Savia is Conductor Laureate of the Evansville Philharmonic Orchestra, following a thirty-one year tenure as Music Director of the Evansville Philharmonic beginning in 1989. Recently appointed Artistic Advisor and Principal Guest Conductor of the Indianapolis Opera, Savia also served as Associate Conductor of the Indianapolis Symphony Orchestra from 1990-1996, and has guest-conducted throughout North and South America and around the globe. A native of Livingston, New Jersey, Savia graduated from Butler University's Jordan College of the Arts. He has recorded Russell Peck's The Thrill of the Orchestra with London's Royal Philharmonic Orchestra and Ottorino Respighi's Piano Concerto with pianist Antonio Pompa-Baldi and the Evansville Philharmonic Orchestra. A 2005 production of Brundibar garnered unparalleled local, regional, and national attention through a featured story on CNN. Savia's innovative programming skills and his ability to connect with audiences everywhere have been documented in profiles in Musical America and Symphony Magazine. Maestro Savia was the recipient of the 2004 Mayor's Arts Award.

The career of lifelong Evansvillian **Jon Michael Siau** spans 42 years as art educator and coach with the EVSC. In 1999, USA Today named him to the All-USA Teacher Team, the only art teacher so recognized. His illustrations commissioned by the United States Olympic Committee have been viewed worldwide. In 2016 he published "The Life and Times of a Harper Hornet," an autobiography from which this selection is taken. The following year he co-produced (with music by John Michael O'Leary) the song, "I Will Never Forget the Words You Never Said."

Nicolette Soulia is an ESL and creative writing instructor, author of short fiction and poetry, and dog-mom to a rambunctious Siberian husky. Her writing tackles themes of mental illness, trauma, resilience, and love. She is the author of the poetry collection, *It Started With Linguine*, and she has also appeared in *Open Door Poetry Magazine* and the poetry competition series *Fire to the Mic: Season 1*. She is currently working on her second poetry collection and her first flash fiction anthology. She resides in Evansville, Indiana, and you can find her on IG, Twitter, & Tiktok @nicolettesoulia, and on Facebook @ Nicolette Soulia Poetry.

Dr. Kristen Strandberg is a musicologist and the Assistant Director of Online Learning at the University of Evansville. She graduated with a B.M. in cello performance from the University of Minnesota and earned her PhD in musicology at Indiana University. She came to UE in 2017 as Assistant Professor of Music History and taught a course in 2019 on "Music in Evansville from the Civil War to WWII." She has published articles and essays on nineteenth-century music, as well as on music history pedagogy.

Sr. Jeana Visel, OSB, joined the Sisters of St. Benedict of Ferdinand, Indiana, in 2003, making first profession in 2006 and perpetual profession in 2010. A northern Illinois native, she completed a BA in religious studies from Kenyon College and an MA in theology with a concentration in monastic studies from Saint John's School of Theology and Seminary. She earned a Doctor of Ministry in spirituality from The Catholic University of America. She has studied icon painting with master iconographer Xenia Pokrovsky and continues studies with iconographer Marek Czarnecki. She is author of *Icons in the Western Church: Toward a More Sacramental Encounter* (Liturgical Press, 2016). Her musical background includes ten years of voice lessons and choral singing, and several years of chant study and practice, especially with Anthony Ruff, OSB. She is a regular cantor for Monastery Immaculate Conception and Saint Meinrad Archabbey. As Dean of School of Theology Programs and Director of the Graduate Theology Program, she oversees the non-seminary programs at Saint Meinrad Seminary and School of Theology.

This is the first published work by **Carina Wahlstrom**. Previously, she has competed in short story contests such as the Battle the Beast Contest in 2016 and the Irvington Halloween Festival in 2020 (what better year to write a spooky story, right?). She lives in southern Indiana and always listens to the radio in her car.

Christine Wisch is a Ph.D. candidate in musicology with a minor in ethnomusicology at Indiana University, where she has taught graduate and undergraduate music history classes and is a staff member at the Latin American Music Center. She holds bachelor's degrees in Spanish and music education from the University of Houston and a master's degree in musicology from Indiana University. Her work as a musicologist focuses primarily on nineteenth-century Spanish classical music and issues of patronage, nationalism, and Romanticism. A trained violinist and dedicated educator, Christine frequently collaborates on audience engagement projects, ranging from program notes and pre-concert lectures to guided listening activities.

Daniel W. Wright is an award-nominated poet and fiction writer. He most recently wrote the foreword for *Sacred Decay: The Art of Lauren Marx* (Dark Horse, 2021) and is the author of *Love Letters from the Underground* (Spartan Press, 2021), *Brian Epstein Died for You* (Spartan Press, 2020) and *Rodeo of the Soul* (Spartan Press, 2019). His work has appeared in print journals such as *BUK100*, *365 Days*, and *Gasconade Review*, as well as online journals such as *Book of Matches*. His work was recently translated into Russian, and he has served on the board of the literary magazine *River Styx*. He currently resides in St. Louis, MO where you can usually find him in a bar or a bookstore.

Also from Bird Brain Publishing

ODD

NUMBERS

by

M. Grace

Bernardin

Is it possible to find love in the heart of the Midwest between a strip mall and a cornfield? This is the quest of three friends who meet in the 1980s at the Camelot Apartments, located amidst the suburban sprawl of the southern Indiana town of Lamasco.

Frank, who moves from the East coast to Lamasco to start a market research firm, is a well-bred, charming, polished Ivy Leaguer with a penchant for classical music. Vicky, the noisy downstairs neighbor who is constantly trying to drown out Frank's classical music with rock and roll, is a tough-talking, whisky-guzzling, Harley-riding lady bartender from western Kentucky with a reckless spirit and a haunted past.

Between Frank and Vicky is Allison, an image-conscious, self-improvement junkie who gives up a promising marketing career in Chicago to return to her hometown of Lamasco at the urging of her high school sweetheart and fiancé, with whom she has long since fallen out of love.

"In my line of work, you've got to look out for the odd numbers.... Hospitality is what it's all about. A place where everybody feels welcome–no one's left out...maybe we can make little places in the world where all are welcome – even the odd numbers." – Excerpt from the novel

An unusual love story set in the Midwestern southern Indiana town of Lamasco, Odd Numbers is a poignantly witty story of love as three friends seek redemption, restoration, meaning, and belonging in a world of isolation.
– the Publisher

Advance Praise for *ODD NUMBERS*

"Touching, clever, and at times delightfully off the wall, Odd Numbers is a gulp of fresh air. Readers will be hard pressed to remain at arm's length from Vicky, Allison, and Frank, because, after all, they are like us—flawed but hopeful.

"Bernardin's prose reminds me of Willa Cather, her descriptions elegant but not blustery or garish. Those among us who esteem a well-crafted sentence have a new wordsmith to add to our list of favorite writers. Odd Numbers is a finely crafted story of the human heart."
 - Mike Whicker, author of the bestseller, *Invitation to Valhalla* and *Blood of the Reich*

"An inspiring read, courageously honest, and full of hope for all of the flawed...climaxing in a sublime symphony of charity."
 - Judy Lyden, author of *Pork Chops*

The Miracle of Stalag 8A –
Beauty Beyond the Horror
Olivier Messiaen and
the Quartet for the End of Time
by
John William McMullen

"On 15 January 1941, in a German prison camp in Silesia, music triumphed over Time, breaking free of rhythm and liberating a quartet of French prisoners and their listeners from the horrors of their time. The Quartet for the End of Time has earned its place in the canon and history of Western music, but, more important, it has earned its place in our hearts. Its musical beauty, at once terrifying and sublime, exalts listeners and performers alike, and the story of its creators stands as a testament to the powers of music and human will to transcend the most terrible of times." – Rebecca Rischin, Associate Professor, Ohio University School of Music, and author of *FOR THE END OF TIME: THE STORY OF THE MESSIAEN QUARTET* (Cornell University Press, 2003; 2006).

"McMullen's novel is worthy of the Shakespearean phrase, 'if music be the food of love, play on, give me excess of it.' The Miracle of Stalag 8A is a deeply moving piece reminiscent of the dissonant sounds of the quartet itself, which breaks with temporality in order to touch the endless moment of timelessness. Mingled with undying faith in a time of horrors that induced disbelief in many, the music gives us a hope, in the words of the novel, for a 'virginal peace pregnant with possibility'."

– Steven C. Scheer, Ph. D., author of *The Heart Ages, But It Doesn't Grow Old* and *Dancing With the Daffodils*

"World War II engulfed so many and so much in its darkness, and yet its upheaval also called some to create a revelation of faith and hope. As Messiaen's music captures both this desolation and praise, McMullen recreates with simple directness the human situation of Messiaen and his fellow prisoners and their triumphal first performance of this master work of twentieth century music which transcends time." - Rev. Harry Hagan O.S.B., Associate Professor of Scripture, Saint Meinrad Seminary.

"*The Miracle of Stalag VIIIA* points to the way in which the composer's music encapsulated yet transcended its circumstances to speak to people of diverse beliefs, and none."

– Dr. Christopher Dingle, author of *The Life of Messiaen* (Cambridge University Press, 2007).

"The musical world interprets the miracle of Stalag 8A as the perfect performance of the "Quartet for the End of Time" in inhuman conditions by musicians suffering from cold and slow starvation. Most critics will wax rhapsodic as they praise McMullen for building his novel to the crescendo of the premier of the "Quartet," that briefly released both captives and captors from the brutality of their situation and moved them all to silence. However, the miracle that McMullen also subtly chronicles is the coming together as one the four musicians: Messiaen, the faithful-Catholic and mystic composer; Pasquier, the fallen-away Catholic agnostic cellist; le Boulaire, the atheist violinist; and the irrepressible Akoka, warrior Trotskyite Jew and master of the clarinet."

– Phillip E. Pierpont, Ph.D., Professor of English and former Academic Dean, Vincennes University, Vincennes, Indiana

The enigmatic Messiaen, avant-garde composer, devout Catholic, and ornithologist, composes the Quartet in Stalag 8A, transforming man's inhumanity to man with hope. Yet to the avant-garde, he was too traditional and too religious; to the traditionalists and religious, he was too avant-garde. As a result, he will always stand somewhere outside of Time.

– The Publisher

The Last Blackrobe of Indiana and The Potawatomi Trail of Death

From the forgotten history of 1830s Indiana, John William McMullen unearths the true story of Benjamin Petit, a French Attorney turned missionary priest, and his mission to the Potawatomi People in the Diocese of Vincennes, Indiana.

Under the urging of the saintly Bishop Simon Bruté, Petit joined the northern Indiana Potawatomi tribes in 1837, a year before their forced removal west. McMullen retells the incredible journey of Petit who traveled with the Potawatomi People and became part of their history.

"The deportation of Chief Menominee and his tribe of Potawatomi Indians from their reservation at Twin Lakes in Marshall County, in September, 1838, is one of the darkest pages in the history of Indiana. The blood of a helpless people stained the hands of a civilized and Christian state."

– Benjamin Stuart, Indiana journalist, early 20th century

Red Flag and other Poems
by
Tim Heerdink

"The world must heed the warning that comes to us from the victims of the Holocaust and from the testimony of the survivors. In the face of great suffering and horror, our initial inclination is silence and proclaiming 'never again.' Yet that is not enough. We must maintain a constant vigil against evil that degrades or denies the human dignity of any human person or persons. Tim Heerdink's Red Flag and Other Poems calls us to examine our own silence in the face of old hatreds and renewed prejudices in the 21st century."

- The Publisher

"A call to action, urging us not to turn a blind eye to red flags or forget the history behind us. A stark reminder of the Holocaust and a warning of lurking dangers with technology and politics."

- Jenna Citrus, author of *An Opened Book End*

Tadpoles by **Joshua Britton**

Two boys plan to sell the tadpoles they find in a creek to pet stores after they turn into frogs; a pianist tries to protect his infant child from becoming collateral damage when his neighbor falls afoul of the mob; a volatile father, released from institutionalization, tries to convince his in-laws that he is fit to take care of his two-year-old son; worrying about how to tell his conservative parents that his girlfriend is pregnant, a man finds the remains of a corpse in her backyard.

Twelve tales of children struggling with childhood, and parents grappling with parenthood, told with wit and sympathy.

"These stories, artfully told, are replete with conflicted persons in complex situations. What an engaging read! Joshua Britton has a great way of laying out a story that leads the reader in. He offers much to lovers of short fiction."
- Frank Gordon, author of *Somewheres in the Middle*

"Joshua Britton's *Tadpoles* captures shots like a hidden photographer documenting the first steps of children to their inevitable mistakes. These collected stories take the reader from the eyes of a kid to parents and guardians across genres of drama, crime, dystopia, and the apocalyptic."

- Tim Heerdink, author of *Red Flag and Other Poems*, *Razed Monuments* and *The Human Remains*

"Britton's works are fresh, bright, and at times stark, pungent, and dark. His stories cover themes of life and death, childhood happiness and teenage angst, making friends to the era of friend requests, ranging from creeps and corpses to tadpoles and spiders. A unique voice –the likes of John Updike and Walker Percy."

- The Publisher

www.ingramcontent.com/pod-product-compliance
Lightning Source LLC
Chambersburg PA
CBHW032035240626
47154CB00003B/923